SUCCI
ON THE I

Based on an Analysis of 22 Seasons actual results.

by

Simon Carrley

The book to help you win Dividends
How to find Score Draws right through the season
Wide variety of example entries for all
A genuine aid for everyone

Published by   *Casdec Ltd*
22 Harraton Terrace
Birtley
Chester le Street
Co. Durham
DH3 2QG
Tel: (091) 410 5556

NOTE ON STAKING COSTS

READERS PLEASE NOTE

All stakes in example entries are for illustration only. Please check your coupon for stake revisions before completing your entry.

First Printing August 1991
Reprinted September 1991

ISBN 0 907595 70 7

"Success on the Pools"!

will help you get a.....

and the joy of a lifetime

"Success on the Pools"!............

.......a great way to make a living

by Simon Carrley

CONTENTS

Page

Introduction 4

Summary of 22 Seasons Score Draws 5

Basic Statistical Summary.................................6

Overview of the 6 Score Draw Tables...............8

Permutations : An Overview........................... 11

Basic Permutation Table.................................13

Non-Consecutive Permutation Table.............. 15

The Tables: ... Table One 16

.... Table Two.............................. 22

.... Table Three.......................... 29

.... Table Four............................34

.... Table Five 51

.... Table Six............................. 62

Using the Tables in combinations.................. 71

Other methods of draw selection................... 80

Permutations 89

Perms and actual entries............................... 97

Notes on entries 99

Example entries 100

Larger entries : Mixed approaches............... 130

Ways and Means.. 149

Yes, but it's fun isn't it?............................... 150

Appendix - Table Six revised to end of
    Season 1991 151

And finally.. 156

INTRODUCTION

Here at last is a Football Pools book with a difference. It combines the two main features of interest to everyone who sends in their weekly or standing entry, or belongs to a syndicate or whatever. Those two main features are:

- Clear pointers on the selection of potential Score-Draws;
- Guidance on permutations and other methods of entry.

The six tables in the book give clear selection pointers from different view points. All Tables have guidance notes and can easily be used alone or in various combinations. There are no restrictions on the number of selections, which entry (e.g. permutation) to use or how much to invest. Whatever your present approach, you should find one or more of the Tables directly useful to you.

The book, and in particular the Tables, springs from an in-depth analysis of Score-Draw patterns (on coupons) over 22 consecutive seasons. The resulting trends including both coupon numbers and actual team performance, are presented in simplified form in the Tables. Taken with the other information and permutation guidance - plus examples - given in the book, this means that both "Beginner" and "Expert" will find something of interest, enabling them to improve the quality of their entries.

The purpose of sending in an entry is to win dividends, and hopefully to "Hit the Jackpot". The purpose of this book is to help you do just that, by reducing the odds against you. The original information contained in the Tables, combined with sensible entries is aimed at increasing **your** chances of being a winner.

SUMMARY OF 22 SEASONS COUPON SCORE-DRAWS

All of the main selection Tables in this book (with the exception of Table 6) are based entirely on actual coupon Score-Draws over 22 consecutive seasons. The term "Coupon Score-Draws" means matches resulting in a Score-Draw - which were included in pools coupons over the period of 22 years. All other results, such as mid-week matches, replays etc. are excluded from the figures. You therefore have the certainty that the Tables are a true reflection of actual coupon-match results (i.e. Score-Draws).

Table 6 is based on actual **Team** draw performance over 11 years, covering both Score and No-Score draws.

It is of course a fact that any match can be affected by a host of factors including climate, team changes, quality of management, position in the league, recent performance, personality problems and so on. But do remember that the 22 season statistics which follow - and the Tables - are **actual** results, i.e. they incorporate all the above factors. In plain English, they have occurred despite or perhaps because of, the thousand and one things which can and do affect the outcome of a game.

The Tables give clear pointers to potential Score-Draws for the whole season. Your interest is naturally in these pointers because one or more of the Tables will aid **your** selection preferences, whether or not you include other elements of your own choice. But do look at the summary which follows; it shows the extent to which analysis has been applied to actual results which are then translated into the Tables.

BASIC STATISTICAL SUMMARY

All figures apply to the standard coupon numbers, i.e. 55, increased to 58 since 1985 season.

1.	Total Score-Draws	8608	
2.	Total weeks	845	
3.	Total seasons	22	
4.	Total numbers 55 (to 1985), 58 from 1986		
5.	Average Score-Draws per season	391	(Rounded)
6.	Average Score-Draws per week	10	
7.	Average Score-Draws per coupon number	154	(55 numbers)
		148	(58 numbers)
8.	Average Score-Draws per number, per season	7	(Rounded)
9.	Average Score-Draws per number, per week	0.18	

For those who revel in statistics, let me caution against in-depth cross-comparison of the above figures. It is possible to work out various relationships between totals and averages, and to give undue focus to the change from 55 to 58 numbers. The latter change increased the odds against you - the reader - quite dramatically. The Tables in this book aim to help you put the odds on your side. It is to the Tables that your attention should be directed. The above summary is the "Baseline" information only.

NOTES (on Page 6)

ITEM 1:   *All coupon Score-Draws over 22 consecutive seasons.*

ITEM 2:   *All weeks in 22 consecutive seasons.*

ITEM 3:   *Self-explanatory.*

ITEM 4:   *The Tables take account of the change from 55 to 58 numbers.*

ITEM 5:   *Item 1, divided by Item 3.*

ITEM 6:   *Item 1, divided by Item 2.*

ITEM 7:   *Item 1, divided by 55/58.*

ITEM 8:   *Item 5, divided by 55/58*   The difference in result is minimal

ITEM 9:   *Item 6, divided by 55/58*   and has been rounded.

ITEM 9 is meant to show the average chance of any number producing a Score-Draw in any week, based on 10 Score-Draws per week.

OVERVIEW OF THE SIX TABLES

The main aids to selecting potential Score-Draws are the six Tables which follow this overview. There are other "Selection Pointers" given, but these latter are there to prompt your own thinking; in other words to widen your knowledge and understanding of Score Draw selection methods. One person's simple idea can be adapted by others and if the result is an improvement in selection success, so much the better!

The same reasoning applies to the six Tables. Suggestions for their use in actual entries on coupons (i.e. as a basis for selecting however many matches you want to cover) are given. Individual readers will, however, - and rightly - think of other ways of using the Tables either singly or in combinations as the basis of their selections.

In brief, the six Tables provide:

Table One	Score-Draw performance by coupon number over 22 seasons, in merit order. This is a simple table for quick entry purposes (22 seasons).
Table Two	Score-draw performance by Division (or Groups) with merit order shown within each group (22 seasons). Ideal for those who like to spread selections down the coupon.

| Table Three | Score-Draws by Sequence, i.e. best performers for the 1st Score Draw, the 2nd Score Draw, the third and so on up to the 12th Score Draw. For each of these sequences, "Next Best" selections are shown. This Table will be of great interest to most readers (22 Seasons). |

| Table Four | Score-Draws by Pairs, i.e. the best performing pairs - using any combination on the coupon - shown in merit order. This Table will be of real value to those who like to use pairs either for part or all of their entry (22 seasons). |

| Table Five | Score Draws by Season Weeks, i.e. the best and worst performers in the 1st, 2nd, 3rd, (etc.) weeks of the season. Very useful for those who vary their entry from week to week (22 Seasons). |

| Table Six | Score-Draws by Teams. This gives a clear rating for every team in the 4 main Divisions and the Scottish Premier Division. Ratings for both Home and Away are given, and also cover No-Score Draw and All Draws performance. A real aid for those who want to focus on actual teams in any week (11 Seasons). |

You will see from the above that individual Tables can be used on their own. Equally, many combinations are possible, e.g. using two or more Tables to form the basis of selections. The exception to this is that Tables One and Two cannot be effectively used together because their base is the same, i.e. they are derived from the same figures. All other Tables have different bases and can therefore be combined as the reader wishes.

Tables One to Four are useful for either weekly **or** standing entries. Tables 5 and 6 are meant for weekly entries only. It really is worth your while to study the Tables carefully and to consider how the information they provide can best be used to help **you** with your selection process. You will find the Notes on each Table, and the examples given about using the Tables, helpful in this process. And you have the knowledge that **ALL** the Tables rest entirely on actual results over a long time period. This makes the pointers they give of real value, based on fact, not "Systems".

PERMUTATIONS : AN OVERVIEW

To be a winner, two things are needed. Sound selections is one of those essentials. A good entry which maximises your chances (at a reasonable cost) of getting successful selections on one line is the other. Most entries are based on perms, with which most readers will be familiar.

In the main section on Permutations, guidance is given on both "Full Cover" and "Conditional Guarantee" perms and on other methods of entry. And each of the main Tables is followed by examples of how to use the pointers provided (i.e. the selections) in various ways.

For now, it is enough to make a few basic points:

- Full Cover perms are best, but can be costly. See the table on page 13 for the number of lines needed to cover eight from between 9 and 20 selections.

- Conditional Guarantee perms are worthwhile but only if the perm provides for eight correct on a line if the conditions are met.

- Other methods of entry such as Block Perms and Pairs can also be very useful. Again, examples are given later.

Individual readers will of course have their own ideas about preferred entry methods. It is therefore right to emphasise that examples and suggested entries are meant to be nothing more than what they are, i.e. examples and suggestions. But even the knowledgeable reader may find something of value in the guidance given about perms. The crucial point may be obvious, but is worth stating: there is little point in spending time and thought on making your selections and then to waste money on a weak form of permutation or other entry method. Use of the Tables or other pointers should improve your chances of success. Make the best of that chance by ensuring your entry is a good one.

There is a commonly held belief - and practice - of using the same selections and entry method every week. What's wrong with that? In short, NOTHING! If that practice suits your inclination, then so be it. But do remember that with very cheap entries available on low cost pools you can do both, i.e. put in your standard entry **and** use a different entry on another coupon or even on your usual pools form. Ultimately, the choice is yours. What matters is that you **think** about your choice and then make the most of it. That's a step in the right direction, which is a dividend cheque in the post!

BASIC PERMUTATION TABLES

The Table below shows the number of lines needed to cover any number up to 8, from up to 20 selections.

Any From	2 No's or Groups	3 No's or Groups	4 No's or Groups	5 No's or Groups	6 No's or Groups	7 No's or Groups	8 No's or Groups
3	3	1	-	-	-	-	-
4	6	4	1	-	-	-	-
5	10	10	5	1	-	-	-
6	15	20	15	6	1	-	-
7	21	35	35	21	7	1	-
8	28	56	70	56	28	8	1
9	36	84	126	126	84	36	9
10	45	120	210	252	210	120	45
11	55	165	330	462	462	330	165
12	66	220	495	792	924	792	495
13	78	286	715	1287	1716	1716	1287
14	91	364	1001	2002	3003	3432	3003
15	105	455	1365	3003	5005	6435	6435
16	120	560	1820	4368	8008	11440	12870
17	136	680	2380	6188	12376	19448	24310
18	153	816	3060	8568	18564	31824	43758
19	171	969	3876	11628	27132	50388	75582
20	190	1140	4845	15504	38760	77520	125970

NOTES

Using the above table: Read **across** the top line for the number to be covered (or permed) from the list of numbers in the left-hand column (3 to 20) **downwards**. When the figures meet, the result is the total of lines required.

Examples: 1 - To cover 4 numbers or groups from 8, requires 70 lines.

2 - To cover 8 numbers or groups from 13, requires 1287 lines.

Mention of "Groups" is deliberate; using groups is dealt with later in the section about Permutations. So, to cover any 2 groups from 7 groups (e.g. groups of 4 matches) requires 21 combinations, and to cover 4 groups from 10 groups requires 210 combinations.

The table on page 13 refers to "Full Cover" permutations because the given number of lines includes all possible combinations. Other forms of permutations are explained later.

›› SOCCER SCORES ‹‹

FOOTBALL
RESULTS England
win again

NON-CONSECUTIVE CALCULATION TABLE

The Table below shows the number of lines needed to cover any number up to 8 on a non-consecutive basis, from up to 20 selections.

Any From ↓	2 No's or Groups	3 No's or Groups	4 No's or Groups	5 No's or Groups	6 No's or Groups	7 No's or Groups	8 No's or Groups	Examples
3	1	-	-	-	-	-	-	
4	3	-	-	-	-	-	-	Any 4 from
5	6	1	-	-	-	-	-	12 with no 2
6	10	4	-	-	-	-	-	consecutive
7	15	10	1	-	-	-	-	selections,
8	21	20	5	-	-	-	-	needs 126
9	28	35	15	1	-	-	-	lines.
10	36	56	35	6	-	-	-	
11	45	84	70	21	1	-	-	Any 8 from
12	55	120	126	56	7	-	-	19 with no 2
13	66	165	210	126	28	1	-	consecutive
14	78	220	330	252	84	8	-	selections
15	91	286	495	462	210	36	1	needs 495
16	105	364	715	792	462	120	9	lines,.
17	120	455	1001	1287	924	330	45	
18	136	560	1365	2002	1716	792	165	Any 2 non
19	153	680	1820	3003	3003	1716	495	consecutive
20	171	816	2380	4368	5005	3432	1287	groups (of any size) from 10 groups, needs 36 combinations

Note: Read across and down, where lines meet, that is the total you need.

THE TABLES : TABLE ONE

Now you know what this book is about, what the Tables cover, and that there is more information about permutations plus other guidance to help you become a winner. It's time to get to the substance or main content, the first part of which is focused on selecting potential Score-Draws.

Table One is a simple straightforward record of Score Draw performance by coupon number over the whole period since they were first introduced. All coupon numbers are shown in merit order, i.e. the best performing number is shown ranked as 1, the next best as 2 etc. Where numbers have the same performance figure, they are equally ranked.

The percentage figure shown against each number is that number's share of the **total** Score Draws. Similarly, the percentage of weeks column shows the frequency with which each coupon number produced a Score Draw based on the total of weeks over the whole period.. The higher the percentage, the better the performance; that sounds obvious, but it is worth pointing out that a percentage figure of 20 or more means that you can expect a Score Draw in about one week in five or slightly better. Linking this to sequence tables published in the daily papers - usually mid-week - where actual matches due for a Score-Draw can be identified, is not difficult. Where both the actual match and the coupon number are in the "Due for a Score Draw" category, it is worth including that match/number in your entry.

Of course it is quite possible to use the Table on its own. It has stood the test of time; the top twenty numbers have consistently produced very close to 40% of ALL coupon Score Draws in the whole period. Is that significant? Well, look at it this way. Twenty numbers out of 58 on the coupon represents less than 35% of the total numbers, but provides nearly 40% of the required result, i.e. Score Draws. That puts the odds on your side and the wise person knows that that is the way to bet.

Note that numbers 56 - 58 have been in use since 1985/6, but have done well in Score Draw results. Therefore it is worth including one or more of these in your entry.

Table One can be used as it stands, or in conjunction with other Tables (except Table Two, which uses the same base figures). You have in this Table a quick and easy way of identifying however many selections you want for your weekly or standing entry.

TABLE ONE: SCORE-DRAWS BY COUPON NUMBER IN MERIT ORDER

Coupon No'	Total Score Draws	% of Overall Total	% of Weeks	Rank	Coupon No's	Total Score Draws	% of Overall Total	% of Weeks	Rank	
15	188	2.18	22.	1	35	153	1.77	18.1	18	
28	180	2.09	21.3	2	43	153	1.77	18.1	18	
2	179	2.04	20.8	3	50	153	1.77	18.1	18	
39	176	2.04	20.8	4	20	152	1.76	18.00	19	
16	172	2.00	20.3	5	24	152	1.76	18.00	19	
19	171	1.98	20.2	6	9	151	1.75	17.8	20	
30	168	1.95	19.8	7	34	151	1.75	17.8	20	
10	167	1.94	19.7	8	48	151	1.75	17.8	20	
11	167	1.94	19.7	8	36	150	1.74	17.7	21	
17	167	1.94	19.7	8	37	148	1.71	17.5	22	
29	165	1.91	19.5	9	14	147	1.70	17.4	23	
12	163	1.89	19.3	10	26	147	1.70	17.4	23	
8	162	1.88	19.2	11	32	146	1.69	17.2	24	
40	161	1.87	19.00	12	22	145	1.68	17.1	25	
6	161	1.87	19.00	12	41	144	1.67	17.00	26	
13	160	1.85	18.9	13	49	144	1.67	17.00	26	
21	160	1.85	18.9	13	3	143	1.66	16.9	27	
27	160	1.85	18.9	13	31	143	1.66	16.9	27	
45	160	1.85	18.9	13	52	143	1.66	16.9	27	
23	159	1.84	18.8	14	54	141	1.64	16.6	28	
47	159	1.84	18.8	14	25	139	1.61	16.4	29	
51	158	1.83	18.7	15	46	139	1.61	16.4	29	
42	157	1.82	18.2	16	53	137	1.59	16.2	30	
1	157	1.82	18.6	16	44	132	1.53	15.6	31	
38	154	1.78	18.2	17	55	130	1.51	15.4	32	
18	154	1.78	18.2	17	4	129	1.49	15.2	33	
5	154	1.78	18.2	17	58	38	38%	24.5	34	4
7	153	1.77	18.1	18	56	34	34%	21.9	35	Seasons
33	153	1.77	18.1	18	57	28	28%	18.0	36	Only

Notes: The Total Score-Draw column shows the "Performance" of each coupon number. The Overall Total column shows the percentage figure from the grand total of all coupon Score-Draws (8608).

The Weeks column shows the percentage figure from the grand total of all coupon weeks (845).

Example: Coupon No.15 produced 188 Score-Draws over 22 seasons. This represents over 2% of **all** coupon Score-Draws. No.15 was a Score-Draw in over 22% of all coupon weeks, i.e. just over 1 week in 5. No. 15 therefore ranks as 1, the top performance. The top 20 in this Table produced nearly 40% of all Score-Draws in the 22 Season period.

USING TABLE ONE

The most obvious way of using Table One is the good old "Any 8 from the top 10 or 12 or whatever" depending on how many selections you want to cover and what stake you can afford. The Table is ideal for the quick and easy method of selection, and for either weekly or standing entries.

Commonsense dictates that it is perhaps unlikely that 8 Score Draws will turn up in the same week, all in the top 10 or 12 selections. And if they do, they are likely to occur in a week when there are a number of other Score-Draws on the coupon. These considerations may not be significant to the person in a hurry. To others, who want every entry to aim directly at the elusive high dividend, using Table One will merit a little more thought.

Possibilities to consider should in my view include:

- A wide spread of selections, covered perhaps in groups, and using whichever perm you choose, but preferably one in which there is a good overall guarantee. Full perms e.g. 8 from 10, or 11 or 12 are of course the best in this respect.

- Watching the sequences. The use of sequence tables from the dailies has already been mentioned. Using coupon number sequences, i.e. watching for those numbers which have not produced a Score Draw for X weeks is another common practice which with the Table One pointers may provide some worthwhile selections.

- Linking Table One to other Tables and using those numbers which are common to two or more, is likely to increase your chances of success. If you dislike putting all your faith (and your stakes!) in numbers alone, a combination of pointers from both Tables One and Six may suit your needs.

In line with the above, if - for example - you want 16 selections, take the top 30 from Table One and the top 30 from Table Six; use the best or highest rated 16 selections from this combination.

Remember that virtually any number of selections can be used in various ways, e.g. 20 selections can be:

- 10 pairs (possibly used as any 4 pairs from 10 pairs = 210 lines).

- 5 Groups of 4 (e.g. any 3 groups from 5 groups = 10 entries of 12 matches each).,

- 4 Groups of 5 (e.g. any 2 groups from 4 groups = 6 entries of 10 matches each).

See also the section on permutations including block entries etc.

THE TABLES : TABLE TWO

This Table uses the same base figures as Table One, but with a vital difference. Table Two shows Score Draw performance by coupon number, within groups or divisions. With 58 numbers on the coupon, the groups cannot be exactly equal. There are five groups in all, covering:

Group 1: Match numbers 1 to 12 inclusive.
Group 2: Match numbers 13 to 24 inclusive.
Group 3: Match numbers 25 to 36 inclusive.
Group 4: Match numbers 37 to 47 inclusive.
Group 5: Match numbers 48 to 58 inclusive.

For **each** of the above groups, the total of all Score Draws in the group is shown. Numbers within the group are then ranked against the group total. This readily identifies the best performers within each group. The Table is therefore ideal for those who want to spread their selections down the coupon.

How well has this Table performed over the 22 season period? Below is the percentage of success for the Top 2, 3 and 4 selections in each group:

	(1-12)	(13-24)	(25-36)	(37-47)	(48-58)	
Group -	1	2	3	4	5	Overall
Top 2	18.3%	18.6%	18.7%	20%	24.7%	16.1%
Top 3	27.2%	27.5%	27.6%	29.5%	36.7%	25.6%
Top 4	35.8%	36.2%	36.2%	38.9%	48.2%	34.8%

It is of course for the user to decide how many selections to take from each group, and ultimately, how to cover those selections with a chosen perm or other entry method. Again, it is worth pointing out that numbers 56-58 have done well since they were brought into use on coupon, and their inclusion in your entry should be considered.

Many readers will have already thought of variations in the make-up of groups. The layout of Table Two shows how to re-use Table One figures to form your own groups and in effect to construct your own Table. For the record, all other Tables have different bases; Table Two can therefore be used either alone or in conjunction with other Tables (i.e. 3 to 6) as the reader wishes. Whatever your choice, Table Two provides an easy source of however many selections you need.

TABLE TWO : SCORE DRAWS BY GROUPS/DIVISIONS IN MERIT ORDER

GROUP ONE : NUMBERS 1 - 12 INCLUSIVE

Coupon No.	Score Draws	% of Total	Rank '	Notes
2	179	9.5	1	Total Score-Draws
10	167	8.8	2	In this Group
11	167	8.8	2	= 1886. All
12	163	8.6	3	percentages are of
8	162	8.5	4	this figure.
6	161	8.5	5	
1	157	8.3	6	1886 = 21.9%
5	154	8.1	7	of the total
7	153	8.1	8	of all coupon
9	151	8.0	9	Score Draws, i.e.
3	143	7.6	10	8608
4	129	6.8	11	

GROUP TWO : NUMBERS 13 - 24 INCLUSIVE

Coupon No.	Score Draws	% of Total	Rank '	Notes
15	188	9.7	1	
16	172	8.9	2	Total Score-Draws
19	171	8.8	3	In this Group
17	167	8.6	4	= 1927. All
13	160	8.3	5	percentages are of
21	160	8.3	5	this figure.
23	159	8.2	6	
18	154	8.0	7	1927 = 22.4%
20	152	7.8	8	of all coupon
24	152	7.8	8	Score-Draws, i.e.
14	147	7.6	9	8608
22	145	7.5	10	

TABLE TWO : SCORE DRAWS BY GROUPS / DIVISIONS IN MERIT ORDER

GROUP THREE : NUMBERS 25 - 36 INCLUSIVE

Coupon No.	Score Draws	% of Total	Rank '	Notes
28	180	9.7	1	
30	168	9.0	2	Total Score-Draws in
29	165	8.9	3	This Group = 1855
27	160	8.6	4	All percentages are
33	153	8.2	5	of this figure.
35	153	8.2	5	
34	151	8.1	6	1855 = 21.5% of ALL
36	150	8.0	7	coupon Score-Draws
26	147	7.9	8	i.e. 8608
32	146	7.8	9	
31	143	7.7	10	
25	139	7.5	11	

GROUP FOUR : NUMBERS 37 - 47 INCLUSIVE

Coupon No.	Score Draws	% of Total	Rank '	Notes
39	176	10.4	1	
40	161	9.5	2	Total Score-Draws in
45	160	9.5	3	This Group = 1683
47	159	9.4	4	(11 numbers). All
42	157	9.3	5	percentages are of
38	154	9.1	6	this figure.
43	153	9.0	7	1683 = 19.5% of ALL
37	148	8.8	8	Coupon Score-Draws,
41	144	8.5	9	i.e. 8608.
46	139	8.2	10	
44	132	7.8	11	

TABLE TWO : SCORE DRAWS BY GROUPS / DIVISIONS IN MERIT ORDER

GROUP FIVE : NUMBERS 48 - 58 INCLUSIVE

Coupon No.	Score Draws	% of Total	Rank '	Notes
51	158	12.6	1	
50	153	12.1	2	Total Score-Draws in
48	151	12.0	3	this Group = 1257
49	144	11.5	4	(11 Numbers). All
52	143	11.4	5	percentages are of
54	141	11.2	6	this figure.
53	137	10.9	7	1257 = 14.6% of ALL
55	130	10.3	8	Coupon Score-Draws,
58	38	3.0	9	i.e. 8608
56	34	2.7	10	No's 56-58 =
57	28	2.2	11	4 Seasons only

EXAMPLES/NOTES

1. In Group 1, No.2 produced 179 Score-Draws; this was 9.5% of the **total** Score-Draw figure for Group 1, (1886) and is therefore ranked 1st in the Group.

2. In Group 3, No.29 produced 165 Score-Draws; this was 8.9% of the **total** Score-Draws for Group 3 (1855) and is therefore ranked as 3rd in the group.

The base figures for this Table are the same as those used in Table 1. This is the only occasion on which two Tables have the same base. When using Tables in combinations of 2 or more, do remember that Tables 1 and 2 cannot effectively be used together. All other combinations are NOT affected.

USING TABLE TWO

Many readers will be inclined to use Table Two as a straightforward source of their 10, 12, 14, 16, 18, 20 (or whatever) selections. By taking the top 2 (or 3 or 4, or 5 etc) from each group, it is easily possible to find the required total.

The more discerning reader will realise that inclusion of some of the lower ranked performers should be considered. If for example, they are overdue for a Score Draw as coupon numbers or as actual matches, you may want to put some of them in your total. Equally, you may want to look at other Tables and select those numbers which, although not top-ranked in Table Two, show up well from another viewpoint. Tables 5 and 3 would provide useful sources of such comparisons. And Table Six will of course show the likely actual Team Score-Draw pointers each week. Where such pointers link to low ranked performers in Table Two, it is worth considering the inclusion of such matches in your entry. With these variations available, it is quite easy to use Table Two as the basis of either weekly or standing entries.

It is a regular feature of actual results that occasionally, one of the Divisions will produce no Score Draws at all. In weeks when Score Draws are scarce and dividends are therefore likely to be high - there are often wide gaps between the required three point results. Table Two lends itself to the exclusion of any group of your choice if and when you think that this is the right way to frame your entry. Some readers will want to cover a number of options, particularly on the cheaper pools. Such options might well include: (AS EXAMPLES ONLY):

- 3 Selections from each of all 5 groups = 15 Selections.

- 4 Selections from any 3 groups out of 5 groups = 10 entries of 12 selections each.

- 4 Selections from any 4 groups out of 5 groups = 5 entries of 16 selections each.

The choice of the number of selections can itself be varied. It will often be right to take perhaps only one selection from one group, two or three from another and so on. The strength of Table Two is therefore in its flexibility, i.e. either as a ready-made source of "Instant" selections, or the basis of considered judgement leading to varied use of the information it provides.

THE TABLES : TABLE THREE

This Table takes a quite different approach to analysing results. In simple terms, it deals with Score Draws by sequence. If you think about the way Score Draws appear in results down the coupon, there must be a first, a second, a third and so on down to whatever the final sequence figure is in any particular week. Since the average (of total Score Draws) per week is between 10 and 11, it is worth analysing the overall results down to the 12th Score Draw. What does all this mean in terms of information to help you with your entry? It means that:

● Every week's Score Draws over 22 consecutive seasons has been analysed;

● The analysis focused on which coupon numbers most often provided the 1st Score Draw, the 2nd, the 3rd, and so on down to and including the 12th;

● For each sequence position, the "Next Best" third and fourth best numbers are given.

● You therefore have in one easily read Table, the 4 best pointers for up to 12 Score Draws.

Some numbers appear in different positions against more than one sequence. For example, the same numbers may be "Best" in one sequence position, and either 2nd or 3rd best in another. You will not therefore find 48 different numbers in the Table.

In the 22 seasons analysed, there has never been a week without Score Draws. As few as 3, and as many as 20, but never a week with none. But of course, the weekly total varies over each season. So, while there is a 1st Score-Draw every week (up to now), the same is not true of the 4th Sequence onwards, i.e. the number of weeks in which the 4th and later Sequences appeared, is less than the total of weeks in the whole period. To put that in a rather obvious way, there was as an example a 12th Score Draw in a lot fewer weeks than a 1st or 2nd Score Draw.

Why stop at the 12th Sequence position? Well if there are more than 12 Score Draws, the dividends are paltry. And the point about frequency of appearance applies; the number of occasions on which a 13th or higher sequence Score Draw occurred was low and analysis was therefore not worthwhile.

Numbers 56 to 58 have been in use for a relatively short time. Clearly, this distorts their value in Sequence terms over a 22 season period. As pointed out in previous notes, they have done well in producing Score Draws, and however you use Table Three, you should consider including one or more of the last three coupon numbers in your entry.

TABLE THREE : SCORE DRAWS BY SEQUENCE

Sequence Score Draw	Best Coupon No.	Next Best No.	3rd Best No.	4th Best No.	Notes
1st	1	2	3	5	In some columns, 2 or
(Score Draw)					more numbers are shown,
2nd	6	8	5	11	i.e. are equal in
3rd	15	16	11	12	performance ranking for
4th	16 + 17	15	19	14, 18	the sequence against
				20	which they appear.
					EXAMPLE
5th	19	23 + 25	22	18, 20	Coupon No.6 is the
				27	most frequent
6th	29	26	28	25	provider of the 2nd
7th	30	28 + 31	27, 29	26 + 39	Score-Draw.
			32		
8th	38	37	40	36	No's 23 and 25 are 2nd
9th	45	48	40 + 42	49	Best in providing the
10th	43	46	39	48 + 50	5th Score-Draw.
11th	47	45	49 + 54		
12th	50,53	49	48	47 + 51	No.25 is also 4th Best
	54				for the 6th Score-Draw.

USING TABLE THREE

It is worth reminding you of what Table Three provides. In the simplest possible format, you have clear indicators of the numbers which most frequently produced each of the 1st to 12th Score Draws over a 22 season period. Some rather obvious uses of this information will already be clear to many readers; examples include:

- Taking the "Best Numbers" reading downwards, and using them in either full cover perms of any 8 from 12 (495 lines), or various combinations, e.g. any 4 pairs from different groups of 6 paired numbers; there are 15 numbers, thus allowing for many variations;

- Taking a mix of selections from each column, to provide however many you need for your entry.

- Giving more weight to the "Best Number" column, i.e. including perhaps half of your selections from that column, with the other half from the numbers in the second and third column.

I have referred - on earlier pages - to the discerning reader, who thinks beyond the obvious. Giving just a little thought to the content of Table Three will show other ways of using it. For example, try using a spare or old coupon (numbers only) and put an X against **every** number listed in the table. Two things become apparent:

- You do not have 48 different numbers

- If you correctly X **every** number including of course those which appear in more than one sequence, you can readily identify the useful numbers which turn up twice or more.

Some suggestions will now spring to mind such as using the total of all numbers in groups of perhaps 6 or 8 or whatever, and bringing groups together to form however many entries you want to cover. A variation of this would be to take the TOP 15 in Column 1, add any other numbers which appear twice or more, and use the total as the basis of your perm. A simple alternative would be to use only those numbers which appear twice or more; if you need additional numbers, take them from the 1st Score Draw downwards in Column 1, using Column 2 to 4 only if the Column 1 number has already been used in your total. If elimination is needed, use the Table 2 indicators, or Table 1 if required. And remember that Table Three can be used with any other Table including of course those which follow it.

THE TABLES : TABLE FOUR

This Table takes another quite unique approach to finding patterns or trends in actual results over time. Originally conceived as a Table based on consecutive pairs in merit order (e.g. 1 + 2, 3 + 4, etc), it has been expanded to show the best pairings (for every coupon number) plus the 2nd and 3rd best. To put that in plain terms, the Table shows which number(s) is/are most likely to provide a Score-Draw when the listed coupon number produces that same result.

Points to note about this Table are:

- All coupon numbers are covered including 56 - 58 which have been in use since 1986 only;

- "Best Pair(s)" means the number(s) shown under that heading against the listed coupon number, and indicates the best or most frequent performer(s) for that coupon number in the production of a pair of Score-Draws;

- 2nd and 3rd Best number(s) are those with the next best and 3rd best performance in paired Score-Draw results for each coupon number.

- In all columns for some coupon numbers, there are 2 or more entries shown. This means equal performance for those numbers under the given heading and against the given coupon number.

There is an important point to grasp about the figures. They are not always equal in terms of opposites. You might well or easily assume that if No.4 pairs most frequently with No.7, then 7 should pair most frequently with No.4. The Table shows however, that No.7 pairs best with No.29, with No.4 shown as 3rd best. That is because the 7/29 pairing occurred more often that the 4/7 pairing. Similarly, Coupon No.17 shows 34 as one of its Best pairings, but 34 shows 28 as Best, with 17 as 2nd Best, for the same reason, i.e. frequency of occurrence. In some instances, you will find that the listed Best No. does not appear at all in opposite terms;

Coupon No.3 shows 45 as Best, but 45 does not show 3 at all (it was in fact 4th Best for 45 and was therefore not listed against that number). So do remember that listings are according to actual performance against the given coupon number; some opposites are identical (e.g. 28/34 or 18/45) but others are not.

TABLE FOUR SCORE DRAWS BY PAIRS AND COUPON NUMBERS

THIS PAGE: Coupon Numbers 1 - 8 only

Coupon No.	Best Pair(s)	2nd Best Pair(s)	3rd Best Pair(s)	Notes
1	21	4 7	15 19 36 38	Have you read the notes on Table Four (see previous pages)?
2	16	34	17 54	**Example** For coupon No.2, (when it is a Score Draw), the
3	45	10 28	15 18 27	number most likely to **also** produce a
4	7	1	31	Score-Draw is 16. No.34 is
5	40	49	29 39	next or 2nd Best and 17 and 54
6	17	40	10 21 47	are 3rd Best for coupon No.2
7	29	36	4 15	
8	36	15 22	14 28	

TABLE FOUR SCORE DRAWS BY PAIRS AND COUPON NUMBERS

THIS PAGE: Coupon Numbers 9 - 16 only

Coupon No.	Best Pair(s)	2nd Best Pair(s)	3rd Best Pair(s)	Notes
9	33 40	29 34	41	Example For coupon No.13, (when it is a Score Draw), the numbers most likely to also produce the same result are 7 and 17. Nos. 38 and 40 are 2nd Best, and 46 is 3rd Best, for pairing with No.13.
10	6 21	48	29 51 55	
11	37	17	12 28 33	
12	30	21	46 51 53 54	
13	7 17	38 40	46	
14	51	8 15 24	10 21	
15	17	54	7	
16	54	2 50	23 39 40 49	

TABLE FOUR SCORE DRAWS BY PAIRS AND COUPON NUMBERS

THIS PAGE: Coupon Numbers 17 - 24 only

Coupon No.	Best Pair(s)	2nd Best Pair(s)	3rd Best Pair(s)	Notes
17	6 34 15 50 22	55	31	Example Coupon No.17 shows 5 numbers (6, 15, 22, 34 and
18	45	40	17 28 33	50) all as equal Best in producing a Score-Draw when No.17 produces
19	21 54	47	1 10 30 13 53	that same result. No. 55 is 2nd best and 31 is 3rd best for pairing with
20	28	12 49 50 52	2 17 36 39 40	No.17
21	51	12	6 10	
22	17	34 39	8	
23	28	16 25	8 32 40	
24	33	38 39	14 53	

TABLE FOUR SCORE DRAWS BY PAIRS AND COUPON NUMBERS

THIS PAGE : Coupon Numbers 25 - 32 only

Coupon No.	Best Pair(s)	2nd Best Pair(s)	3rd Best Pair(s)	Notes
25	23	21	40 53	Consecutive Pairs (e.g. 1 and 2, 2 and 3, 3 and 4 etc.) are listed separately following this Table.
26	40	24	6 34 50 51	
27	15	31 44	10 21 28 47	
28	34	23	40	
29	7	15	5 37 9 41 10 50 33 53	
30	12	47 51	53	
31	17 28	7 39	12 21 27 7	
32	12	23	17 28 47	

TABLE FOUR SCORE DRAWS BY PAIRS AND COUPON NUMBERS

THIS PAGE: Coupon Numbers 33-40 only

Coupon No.	Best Pair(s)	2nd Best Pair(s)	3rd Best Pair(s)	Notes
33	24	9 15 39	29 37	
34	28	17	22 39 50	
35	17	28 34 55	10 39 42	
36	7 8	21 53 54	1 28 42 49	
37	47	6 21 45 50	29 33	
38	24	13	42	
39	50	22 34	24	
40	5	6 18 28 49	12 18 42 50 51	

TABLE FOUR SCORE DRAWS BY PAIRS AND COUPON NUMBERS

THIS PAGE: Coupon Numbers 41 - 48 only

Coupon No.	Best Pair(s)	2nd Best Pair(s)	3rd Best Pair(s)	Notes
41	28	12 42	6 29 30 53	
42	40 49	41	38	
43	6 12 15	47 54	2 16 39 46 51	
44	17 27	8	22 31 48	
45	18	34 55	28 37	
46	12 49	54	13	
47	30 37 54	6 12	19	
48	6 10 52	12 28 30 45 53	15 21 22 42 51	

TABLE FOUR SCORE DRAWS BY PAIRS AND COUPON NUMBERS

THIS PAGE: Coupon Numbers 49 - 58 only

Coupon No.	Best Pair(s)	2nd Best Pair(s)	3rd Best Pair(s)	Notes
49	54	40 46 50	12 42	
50	17 39	34 49	16 40 54	
51	21	12 30	40	
52	48	30 20 40	7 29 46 50 53	
53	12	30 40	7 29 15 36 24,41,48	
54	49	12 16 15 47	50	
55	17	45	15	
56	34	10 15 41	45	
57	43	9 30 15 34 27 50	6 48 56	
58	10	34	18 22	

TABLE 4 : CONSECUTIVE PAIRS : IN MERIT ORDER

Listed below are the consecutive pairs in merit order, for the benefit of readers who prefer to use one or more such pairs in their entry. No consecutive pair is shown in the main listings for Table Four on previous pages. In other words, none were among the top performers, and only a very few appear in 2nd or 3rd best columns. Equal ranking means equal performance.

Pair	Rank	Pair	Rank
14 + 15	1	6 + 7	11
11 + 12	2	7 + 8	11
15 + 16	3	19 + 20	11
49 + 50	4	32 + 33	11
16 + 17	5	30 + 31	12
41 + 42	5	40 + 41	13
35 + 36	6	46 + 47	13
39 + 40	6	47 + 48	13
12 + 13	6	44 + 45	14
17 + 18	6	45 + 46	14
8 + 9	7	5 + 6	15
10 + 11	7	23 + 24	15
20 + 21	7	25 + 26	15
34 + 35	7	13 + 14	16
50 + 51	7	43 + 44	16
53 + 54	7	48 + 49	16
18 + 19	8	33 + 34	17
26 + 27	8	37 + 38	17
1 + 2	9	4 + 5	18
2 + 3	9	24 + 25	18
31 + 32	9	36 + 37	19
38 + 39	9	51 + 52	19
9 + 10	10	21 + 22	20
27 + 28	10	3 + 4	21
28 + 29	10	22 + 23	22
29 + 30	10	55 + 56	23
42 + 43	10	56 + 57	24
52 + 53	10	57 + 58	25
54 + 55	10		

TABLE FOUR : COMMENTS

The astute reader - which of course means you - will have realised that Table Four is both simple and complex. The simplicity lies in the obvious value of the information laid out in an easy-to-follow way. The complexity lies in part with the sheer volume of work required to analyse results covering all pairings for every week of every season and then putting the results in merit order by coupon number. And in part, the complexity lies in a variety of factors best expressed as questions.

- How does Table Four relate to Table One? In the latter Table for example the top 4 numbers are 15, 28, 2, 39, and yet none of these are linked as Best pairs in Table Four. So frequency of Score-Draw results by individual coupon number is not a pointer to the frequency of paired results, at least up to now.

- What about the frequency of paired occurrences? In other words, why not include for each pair, the number of times it occurred? Doing so would have made the Table more complex in presentation; readers would simply get bogged down in figures and cross comparisons, since in some instances, the 2nd Best pairing(s) for one number would have a higher performance figure than the Best pairing(s) for other numbers, and so on. It is worth pointing out here that a pairing which occurs 3 times in one season (on average) is very good, and that in general, the Best pairings listed by coupon number fall in the "Twice Times Per Season" category.

- Why not list the 4th, 5th, 6th (etc.) best pairing? Again, the result would be literally a barrage of figures, with some rankings having a large batch of pairings shown.

- Why stop at Pairs? Why not an analysis of Threes/Fours/Fives (etc)? Possible yes, practical - well maybe, but not at present, given the time it took to analyse pairs into **their** order of merit by coupon number.

- What about **non**-consecutive pairs? For those devoted to such linkages, you have the consecutive pairings shown separately; all other pairings are by definition, non-consecutive and you need only to study the Table Four pages to check or identify your preferences, if listed.

USING TABLE FOUR

By now, you will - hopefully - have some ideas of your own about the uses of Table Four. I want to point out some aspects of the Table which are worth considering for actual entry purposes. If these pointers are similar to your own conclusions, then well and good. If not, you may gain some ideas and I may be forgiven because the possibilities of Table Four are so varied.

To start with, take the **Best Pair** indicators for **ALL** coupon numbers. Not surprisingly, there are less than 58 different numbers listed because some appear many times as Best pair(s) for different coupon numbers. There are in fact 33 separate numbers listed. In their order of frequency, they are: (No. first, frequency of appearance in Best Pair column, in brackets).

17 (9), 12 (5), 28 (5), 6 (4), 7 (4), 21 (4), 40 (4), 54 (4).
15 (3), 34 (3), 49 (3), 51 (2), 10 (2), 24 (2), 30 (2), 33 (2).
37 (2), 45 (2), 50 (2), 5 (1), 8 (1), 16 (1), 18 (1), 22 (1).
23 (1), 27 (1), 29 (1), 36 (1), 39 (1), 43 (1), 47 (1), 48 (1), 52 (1).

Some readers may want to cover all 33 numbers disregarding pairs entirely. Perms of 8 from 10, or multiple entries of four groups of 3 from 11 groups of 3, plus other methods (e.g. dropping one number, leaving 32 to be covered in 4 groups of 8 or 8 groups of 4, by a wide variety of perms) will spring to mind.

Using the 33 numbers as **PAIRS** means that you must either add another number to make 34 (17 pairs), or drop one number to leave 32 (16 pairs). This may be too expensive for some people, because any 4 pairs from 17 pairs = 2380 lines (or combinations), and any 4 pairs from 16 pairs = 1820 combinations.

Using these approaches, the respective costs are:

Any 4 pairs	Littlewoods	Vernons	Zetters
From 17 Pairs =	£23.80	£6.80	£1.59 (or £2 - 38 Super Stake)
From 16 Pairs =	£18.20	£5.20	£1.22 (or £1 - 82 Super Stake)

NOTE	For Vernons/Zetters, costs are rounded up (to nearest penny). Multiple entries are of course possible on the lower cost pools by making up your 16 or 17 pairs in various ways, perhaps giving more weight to the higher frequency numbers such as 17, 28 etc.

For those who want fewer numbers in their entry, it is quite easy to reduce the above 33 numbers to 19 by dropping those which appear only once in the Best Pair(s) column.

Again, some readers will prefer to either cover all 19 with their favoured perm, or to add or drop one number leaving them with 20 or 18 to cover as they wish. 20 selections can be dealt with as 4 groups of 5, or 5 groups of 4, or 2 groups of 10, or as 10 pairs. In like manner, 18 selections can be seen as 6 groups of 3, or 3 groups of 6, or 2 groups of 9, or as 9 pairs. And full cover perms or other preferred methods can be used to cover any of these combinations.

As pairs, the cost of covering 4 (Pairs) from either 10 (Pairs) or 9 (Pairs) would be (per entry):

	Littlewoods	Vernons	Zetters
10 Pairs =	£2.10	60 p	14 p (or 21p Super Stake)
9 Pairs =	£1.26	36 p	9 p (or 13p Super Stake)

| NOTE | For Vernons/Zetters, costs are rounded up (to nearest penny). |

With costs of the above level, multiple entries are easily possible, particularly as lower cost pools. For Zetters, you would in any case need to spend more, because the single entry costs shown are below the minimum weekly stake.

Another variation in using Table Four is to identify the identical or "True" pairs from the Best Pair(s) column. These are identical or true in the sense that they appear in the Best Pair(s) column as opposites.

Nos 5 and 40 are examples; No.5 appears against 40 and 40 appears against 5, i.e. their performance was identical and Best. There are only 15 pairs in that category; they are (in numerical order):

5 + 40, 6 + 17, 7 + 29, 8 + 36, 12 + 30, 17 + 22, 17 + 50, 18 + 45, 21 + 51, 24 + 33, 28 + 34, 37 + 47, 39 + 50, 48 + 52, 49 + 54.

You may have noticed that only No.17 appears more than once in the given list (it is there 3 times). That means you have 28 different numbers if we leave Pairs aside for the moment. 28 numbers can be dealt with as 2 groups of 14, or 7 groups of 4, or 4 groups of 7, (or 14 pairs). Again a wide variety of full cover perms or other entries can be used on one or more of these combinations. Seen as 14 pairs, costs are:

Any 4 Pairs	Littlewoods	Vernons	Zetters
From 14 Pairs	£10.01	£2.86	67 p (or £1.00 Super Stake)

For the number of lines/combinations or any 4 matches, or groups (including pairs) see the Basic Permutation Table shown earlier.

So far, the uses of Best Pair(s) indicators have been the focus of attention. Some readers will want to extend their interest to 2nd Best or even to 3rd Best indications. It is easy to list all the 2nd Best or even the 3rd Best indications. It is easy to list all the 2nd Best column numbers by frequency of appearance - as was done for Best Pair(s) - and anyone wishing to do so will find 40 numbers shown - with No.34 appearing 6 times, and a small batch of 4 - Time numbers, i.e. 12, 15, 21, 28, 39 and 54. Again, if all the once-only numbers are excluded, the 40 reduces to 22. In numerical order, these 22 are:

6, 7, 8, 12, 15, 17, 21, 22, 23, 24, 28, 34, 38, 39, 40, 45, 47, 49, 50, 53, 54, 55.

Of these 22 numbers, 20 also appear in the Best Pair(s) column, i.e. 6, 7, 8, 12, 15, 16, 21, 22, 23, 24, 28, 34, 39, 40, 45, 47, 48, 50, 54, 55.

The 3rd Best column could be analysed in the same way. These possibilities and the variations they provide make Table Four very flexible and open to interesting uses. I point to this flexibility so as to stimulate **your** thought processes in considering not only this Table, but all the others. You can choose whether or not to use the data provided as it is given, or to apply some thought to going below the surface so to speak, to find ways of using individual or linked Tables which suits your inclination. I am **not** suggesting that every reader needs to be an analyst or spend endless hours in compiling/comparing various combinations of figures from the Tables. The latter are presented in simple, easy to follow layouts precisely to enable readers to use them quickly if they wish. But **some** readers will get a lot of pleasure in thinking about the Tables, possible linkages, new ways of using the information and so on.

I have taken more time and space with Table Four not because it stands above other Tables, but because it provides a good example of variation in use. On average, a single coupon number provides 7 Score-Draws per season. Table Four tells you which pairings are likely to occur between 2 and 3 times per season, for every coupon number. And with the most frequent pairings identified in these pages, your chances of getting 4 pairs together in one week should be improved.

THE TABLES : TABLE FIVE

In Table Five you will find an again quite different approach to selecting potential Score-Draws. With 22 seasons results available, it is - as you have already seen - quite possible to look at those actual records in various ways. This Table takes **individual weeks of the season** as its base. To explain that:

There are usually 39 weeks in the British Football season;

Looking at 22 seasons results of coupon Score Draws, they can be seen as (22) 1st weeks, (22) 2nd weeks, (22) 3rd weeks and so on up to (22) 39th weeks;

The question then becomes: are there numbers which do particularly well in individual weeks of the season? And are there numbers which stand out as low or poor performers in those same individual weeks?

How is the judgement made about good or bad performers? You have seen in earlier pages that on average, any coupon number can be expected to produce between 7 and 8 Score-Draws per season. Since there are 39 weeks in most seasons, that means (on average) one Score Draw in 5 1/2 weeks. Yes, I know that half a week does not exist; think of it as being between 5 and 6 weeks if you prefer that. So in 22 weeks - whether 1st, 2nd, 3rd or whatever - an average of 4 Score Draws per number would be quite acceptable, normal etc. What we are looking for is performance well **above** that average, or well below it, for **each numbered week** of the season. Table Five provides this information.

All season weeks are covered, from 1 to 39. For **each** of those weeks coupon numbers which produced at least 6 Score-Draws are clearly indicated, with the best performers given first. For each of the same weeks, numbers which produced 2 or less Score-Draws are also shown.

51

Do remember that this Table is based on **actual** season weeks by number. This is important because the week number shown on your coupon may **not** be the same as in the Table. For clarity, let me say that week 1 in the Table is the 1st week of the season, Week 2 is the 2nd week and so on, but your coupon may show a different week number. So do make sure you are looking at the correct week when using the Table.

TABLE FIVE : SCORE DRAWS BY SEASON WEEKS WITH HIGH/LOW NUMBERS

THIS PAGE: Weeks 1 to 5 inclusive only

| NOTE | Week numbers read **downwards** on left of page.

Col.A (across) against each week number shows the best numbers.

Col.B (across) shows the poor or low numbers for each week.

Week	
A 6 +	19, 4, 2, 16, 47, 53, 5, 12, 22, 52
1	
B 2-	1, 3, 10, 17, 27, 42, 43, 45, 51, 55, 56, 57, 58
A 6 +	28, 19, 15, 1, 5, 8, 10, 35, 40, 48, 7, 12, 21, 22, 37, 47
2	
B 2-	3, 9, 18, 33, 38, 44, 45, 49, 56, 57, 58.
A 6 +	14, 21, 10, 40, 2, 19, 37, 38, 41, 15, 16, 17, 23, 36, 43
3	
B 2-	8, 13, 20, 33, 49, 52, 55, 56, 57, 58
A 6 +	21, 12, 19, 3, 7, 31, 40
4	
B 2-	2, 13, 16, 18, 23, 26, 35, 36, 41, 46, 47, 48, 50, 56, 57, 58
A 6 +	9, 8, 11, 24, 26, 55
5	
B 2-	14, 15, 17, 19, 22, 23, 25, 29, 36, 37, 42, 44, 47, 48, 49, 52, 56, 57, 58

TABLE FIVE: SCORE DRAWS BY SEASON WEEKS WITH HIGH/LOW NUMBERS

THIS PAGE: Weeks 5 to10 inclusive only

Week	
A 6+ 6 B 2-	13, 16, 49, 2, 30, 53, 55 4, 7, 15, 18, 20, 21, 22, 23, 24, 26, 27, 31, 50, 52, 56, 57, 58
A 6+ 7 B 2-	27, 45, 8, 16, 19, 20, 47, 1, 6, 36, 41, 44 4, 6, 7, 9, 17, 21, 31, 34, 35, 39, 40, 56, 57, 58
A 6+ 8 B 2-	52, 6, 10, 12, 27, 51, 22, 43, 48, 49 3, 14, 19, 20, 25, 26, 30, 32, 36, 40, 47, 50, 56, 57, 58
A 6+ 9 B 2-	45, 3, 6, 54, 17, 18, 28, 30, 38, 47 1, 21, 24, 25, 29, 34, 37, 43, 48, 50, 55, 56, 57, 58
A 6+ 10 B 2-	48, 50, 24, 7, 10, 23, 33, 35, 41, 51, 53 2, 8, 9, 15, 19, 20, 22, 25, 27, 36, 37, 45, 46, 47 56, 57, 58

Example: In Week 9, Coupon No.45 produced 6 or more Score-Draws in the 22 Season period. No.3 likewise, as did No.6. Also in Week 9, Coupon No's 1, 21, 24 etc. produced 2 or less Score Draws.

TABLE FIVE : SCORE DRAWS BY SEASON WEEKS WITH HIGH/LOW NUMBERS

THIS PAGE : WEEKS 11 TO 16 inclusive only

Read **Down** under Week, and **Across** for numbers against A or B

Week	
A 6 +	27, 51, 11, 21, 32, 36, 52, 1, 4, 13, 15, 16, 31, 33, 39
11	
B 2 -	2, 5, 18, 19, 22, 25, 28, 30, 34, 35, 40, 50, 56, 57, 58
A 6 +	12, 6, 17, 28, 55, 45, 47, 2, 9, 12, 6, 46, 48, 49, 53, 54
12	
B 2 -	1, 10, 24, 35, 37, 38, 52, 56, 57, 58
A 6 +	10, 21, 27, 1, 20, 5, 13, 25, 34, 36, 38, 47
13	
B 2 -	11, 12, 18, 37, 48, 49, 53, 56, 57, 58
A 6 +	10, 29, 48, 18, 34, 30, 2, 24, 32, 37, 43, 50, 51
14	
B 2 -	4, 7, 16, 13, 38, 44, 49, 56, 57, 58
A 6 +	30, 48, 24, 9, 16, 22, 26, 34, 35
15	
B 2 -	3, 10, 11, 12, 13, 18, 25, 31, 36, 44, 45, 55, 56, 57, 58
A 6 +	21, 5, 8, 19, 29, 32, 36, 38, 47
16	
B 2 -	3, 4, 8, 14, 15, 45, 48, 49, 50, 56, 57, 58

TABLE FIVE: SCORE DRAWS BY SEASON WEEKS WITH HIGH/LOW NUMBERS

THIS PAGE: Weeks 17 to 20 inclusive only

Week	
A 6+	1, 25, 27, 2, 15, 20, 22, 30, 36, 38, 47
17	
B 2-	5, 7, 8, 21, 23, 46, 48, 49, 50, 56, 57, 58
A 6+	15, 33, 1, 24, 7, 49, 17
18	
B 2-	2, 3, 21, 22, 25, 31, 41, 43, 48, 54, 56, 57, 58
A 6+	43, 40, 42, 28, 31, 36, 51, 15, 16, 23, 26, 30
19	
B 2-	3, 4, 9, 10, 12, 20, 24, 27, 35, 44, 56, 57, 58
A 6+	2, 18, 34, 41, 52, 11, 22, 35, 39
20	
B 2-	3, 4, 6, 25, 27, 30, 44, 47, 48, 56, 57, 58

Reminder: Make sure you are using the correct week number. All Week Numbers used in this Table are based on the actual season weeks which may not correspond with week numbers shown on pools coupons.

TABLE FIVE: SCORE DRAWS BY SEASON WEEKS, WITH HIGH/LOW NUMBERS

THIS PAGE : Weeks 21 - 27 inclusive only

Week	
A 6+ 21 B 2-	9, 15, 13, 7, 30, 38, 1, 2, 8, 18, 25, 27 6, 11, 20, 24, 32, 42, 43, 46, 48, 49, 53, 55, 56, 57, 58
A 6+ 22 B 2-	29, 47, 2, 8, 9, 10, 19, 27, 35, 41, 46, 52 4, 7, 13, 16, 21, 37, 38, 39, 49, 51, 54, 55, 56, 57
A 6+ 23 B 2-	23, 28, 1, 19, 36, 38, 42, 50, 5, 13 4, 6, 14, 22, 41, 43, 44, 45, 52, 53, 56, 57, 58
A 6+ 24 B 2-	6, 7, 10, 11, 17, 28, 34, 42, 1, 4, 15, 24, 29, 50 12, 18, 22, 31, 41, 53, 54, 55, 56, 57, 58
A 6+ 25 B 2-	38, 43, 15, 37, 8, 13, 35, 49, 51 3, 10, 11, 24, 27, 31, 32, 42, 47, 48, 50, 52, 54, 56, 57, 58
A6+ 26 B 2-	16, 27, 39, 6, 9, 23, 26 3, 4, 7, 11, 17, 18, 25, 29, 31, 32, 38, 52, 55, 56, 57, 58
A 6+ 27 B 2-	28, 42, 15, 39, 23, 33, 37, 46 1, 9, 11, 14, 19, 20, 22, 26, 31, 32, 37, 43, 44, 51, 52, 56, 57, 58

TABLE FIVE: SCORE DRAWS BY SEASON WEEKS WITH HIGH/LOW NUMBERS

THIS PAGE: Weeks 28 to 34 inclusive only

Week	
A 6 + 28 B 2-	10, 11, 26, 30, 51, 7, 19, 42, 48, 49, 52 6, 9, 14, 23, 25, 27, 34, 38, 39, 43, 46, 56, 57, 58
A 6 + 29 B 2-	2, 22, 42, 43 1, 4, 5, 7, 8, 9, 13, 14, 16, 20, 21, 30, 31, 32, 36, 38, 44, 45, 50, 51, 52, 58 - 8
A 6 + 30 B 2-	9, 29, 32, 34, 2, 7, 10, 18, 22 4, 5, 6, 15, 19, 21, 24, 25, 26, 33, 39, 42, 46, 51, 53, 54, 55, 56 - 8
A 6 + 31 B 2-	55, 5, 13, 16, 26, 48, 17, 19, 21, 25, 34, 39, 44 4, 9, 29, 32, 33, 46, 49, 52, 56 - 8
A 6 + 32 B 2-	17, 28, 39, 3, 15, 23, 27, 29, 30, 35, 42, 48, 49, 52 2, 4, 5, 9, 10, 19, 21, 43, 44, 46, 51, 55, 56 - 8
A 6 + 33 B 2-	39, 2, 14, 11, 12, 6, 20, 31, 43 1, 3, 9, 24, 32, 36, 40, 41, 47, 56, 57
A 6 + 34 B 2-	51, 23, 28, 43, 1, 3, 9, 15, 16, 25, 27, 32, 45 5, 6, 12, 21, 29, 34, 36, 37, 40, 41, 44, 46, 47, 55, 56 - 8

TABLE FIVE: SCORE DRAWS BY SEASON WEEKS WITH HIGH/LOW NUMBERS

THIS PAGE: Weeks 35 to 39 inclusive

Weeks	
A 6 +	14, 23, 28, 21, 6, 30, 32, 47
35	
B 2-	2, 3, 5, 7, 10, 11, 15, 22, 23, 26, 37, 38, 43, 49, 56 - 8
A 6 +	39, 46, 21, 6, 30, 32, 47
36	
B 2-	2, 3, 5, 7, 10, 11, 15, 22, 23, 26, 37, 37, 43, 49, 56 - 8
A 6 +	45, 23, 39, 49, 37, 40, 41, 44, 50
37	
B 2-	14, 16, 18, 26, 27, 28, 30, 32, 33, 35, 36, 43, 52, 53, 56 - 8
A 6 +	3, 10, 11, 12, 38, 43, 44
38	1, 4, 5, 7, 9, 20, 22, 23, 25, 26, 30, 32, 34, 35
B 2-	39, 40, 48, 51, 52, 56 - 8
A 6 +	NONE!
39	4, 5, 7, 9, 10, 11, 13, 14, 15, 16, 23, 26, 26, 28, 30, 31, 33, 34,
B 2-	35, 38, 39, 40, 43, 44, 45, 46, 49, 50, 51, 52, 53, 54, 55, 56 - 8

USING TABLE FIVE

This Table is clearly most useful in weekly entries which change as the season moves on, since the High and Low indicators differ from week to week. Most readers who are attracted to its use will probably want to take account of both A and B indicators because:

Column A gives the best performing numbers for each week; Column B gives the well below average performers which may be taken as those likely to provide a Score-Draw.

The latter point alone also applies to numbers not listed at all in any given week,i.e. **they** may be seen as even more likely to produce the required result, particularly if well-indicated by other Tables.

Sensible use of Table Five (bearing in mind that the number of high/low indicators varies from week to week) is:

● Always use Column A indicators;

● Make up any required balance from Column B taken with other Tables, particularly Tables 2, 3, and 6.

In some weeks, the use of other Tables will be unavoidable, because the total of indicators is not enough for your entry. This is particularly true in the case of multiple entries which are popular with many people. Most readers will have their preferred method of entry and a favourite full cover or other perm. In such instances, the use of other Tables will help to make up the required total of selections.

What about Standing Entries? A little thought will reveal that Table Five **can** be adapted for such entries. As an example only, assume that a Standing Entry for 14 selections is needed over 10 weeks. Using a sheet of paper or an old coupon (Numbers only), mark the Column A indicators for the chosen 10 week period. Then take the 14 selections which appear most often over the 10 weeks. If elimination is needed, take out those numbers with the least appearances. If extra selections are needed, use Column B indicators with the highest number of appearances over the 10 weeks. And if still in difficulties, use other Tables to either select in or out until you reach 14 selections. You will of course have your own views about the use of Table Five with or without other Tables. My view is that it is at its best when used in combination with other methods.

THE TABLES : TABLE SIX

And now - as the well known saying goes - for something completely different. You have seen in previous Tables how the actual records of coupon number performance can be used to give clear indicators of likely Score-Draws. Many readers will want to base their entry on actual teams/matches playing from week to week, or at least to link their chosen numbers to those matches on their coupons. For them, and for those who like to assess the Draw potential of teams by poring over the form, recent performance, or other factors, Table Six should prove to be of real value.

In brief, this Table:

- Covers the 4 Divisions of the major league plus the Scottish Premier Division. These are the teams which most frequently appear against most of the coupon numbers;

- Shows in a simple format, the Home and Away Draw performance of each team in each Division by ranked merit indicators;

- Ranks the Draw performance of each team, for ALL Draws, No Score-Draws, and Score-Draws, separately.

The lower the ranking (in any column) the better is the performance of the given team. For example, a ranking of 1 under Score-Draws at Home, means that the given team is the best performer under that heading.

Note that for simplicity, equal rankings apply to some teams in some columns. Equal ranking means just that; the given teams have the same performance value under the column heading.

The period covered in this Table is eleven consecutive seasons, i.e. long enough to give reasonable reliability to the rankings. Why not actual figures as well as or instead of rankings? Quite simply, the actual performance figures without rankings would have meant work on your part to identify the likely best selections. And if included with rankings, 6 more columns would be needed, i.e. 3 extra for each of the Home and Away blocks. The given ranking approach coupled with the alphabetical listing of teams in each Division, makes use of the information quick and easy.

Table Six can of course be used on its own. Equally, it can be used with one or more of the other Tables, since all matches appear against a coupon number. Linking the two-teams and numbers - could be the ideal approach for you.

TABLE SIX : DRAW PERFORMANCE RATINGS BY TEAMS

DIVISION ONE

HOME DRAWS   AWAY DRAWS

All Draws	No Score Draws	Score Draws	Teams	Score Draws	No Score Draws	All Draws
8	4	11	Arsenal	13	2	11
13	9	14	Aston Villa	3	12	5
5	8	7	Chelsea	6	10	5
16	3	16	Coventry	14	1	6
10	7	10	Crystal Palace	11	6	12
6	10	4	Derby	6	8	5
3	7	5	Everton	5	11	7
9	2	13	Leeds United	2	2	1
15	11	15	Liverpool	1	5	2
1	1	6	Luton	12	5	13
11	11	8	Manchester City	24	3	15
5	4	9	Manchester United	4	5	3
3	2	8	Norwich	12	7	14
9	3	12	Notts Forest	7	9	8
12	6	14	Queens Park Rangers	25	3	16
6	5	9	Sheffield United	10	4	7
7	10	1	Southampton	1	8	4
2	8	2	Sunderland	9	9	10
14	12	14	Tottenham	8	9	9
4	11	3	Wimbledon	6	8	5

Example	Southampton is best for Home Score-draws.

Liverpool is best for Away Score-draws.

Luton is best for Home No Score-draws.

Leeds United is best for All Away draws.

TABLE SIX : DRAW PERFORMANCE RATINGS BY TEAMS

DIVISION TWO

HOME DRAWS   **AWAY DRAWS**

All Draws	No Score Draws	Score Draws	Teams	Score Draws	No Score Draws	All Draws
5	6	11	Barnsley	2	10	3
8	14	7	Blackburn	1	16	5
7	10	8	Brighton	15	10	17
10	9	16	Bristol City	6	5	5
1	4	5	Bristol Rovers	11	7	10
6	7	11	Charlton	11	15	14
4	2	15	Hull	5	1	2
13	16	14	Ipswich	7	14	11
6	18	3	Leicester	9	16	13
4	1	17	Middlesborough	16	4	16
3	11	4	Millwall	13	6	11
9	11	13	Newcastle	4	6	4
4	1	17	Notts County	8	11	9
2	19	1	Oldham	10	8	10
4	15	2	Oxford	12	12	13
10	13	12	Portsmouth	9	8	7
4	3	12	Port Vale	3	3	1
5	12	6	Plymouth	4	15	8
7	13	7	Sheffield Wednesday	9	13	12
14	7	18	Swindon	13	3	7
11	17	9	Watford	15	13	18
6	5	13	West Bromwich	11	2	6
12	16	11	West Ham	14	9	15
6	8	10	Wolves	11	8	11

Example	Blackburn is best for Away Score-draws.
	Oldham is best for Home Score-draws.

TABLE SIX : DRAW PERFORMANCE RATINGS BY TEAMS

DIVISION THREE

HOME DRAWS   **AWAY DRAWS**

All Draws	No Score Draws	Score Draws	Teams	Score Draws	No Score Draws	All Draws
6	1	14	Birmingham	5	8	3
10	5	12	Bolton	16	7	11
8	4	10	Bournemouth	16	4	10
2	7	3	Bradford City	2	13	2
5	13	2	Brentford	10	8	8
5	4	7	Bury	1	17	6
16	12	11	Cambridge	12	2	5
11	6	12	Chester	13	14	13
1	8	1	Crewe	16	13	14
6	10	4	Exeter	6	9	5
12	12	6	Fulham	10	10	9
9	5	10	Grimsby	8	10	7
6	7	6	Huddersfield	14	10	12
10	11	5	Leyton Orient	6	11	6
7	9	5	Mansfield	11	1	3
9	1	16	Preston	9	12	10
3	8	3	Reading	15	8	11
6	3	9	Rotherham	7	6	4
4	2	8	Shrewsbury	14	5	9
13	7	13	Southend	18	16	15
6	7	6	Stoke	17	3	9
15	8	15	Swansea	15	9	12
17	14	9	Tranmere	3	15	5
14	12	8	Wigan	4	7	1

| Example | Crewe is best for Home Score-draws.
Bury is best for Away Score-draws.
Wigan is best for all Away Draws.

TABLE SIX : DRAW PERFORMANCE RATING BY TEAMS

DIVISION FOUR

HOME DRAWS   **AWAY DRAWS**

All Draws	No Score Draws	Score Draws	Teams	Score Draws	No Score Draws	All Draws
5	5	8	Aldershot	13	11	14
12	7	13	Blackpool	2	7	11
10	4	15	Burnley	9	14	8
5	1	13	Cardiff	18	1	9
11	10	9	Carlisle	16	6	14
16	2	17	Chesterfield	6	3	5
15	9	15	Darlington	7	5	6
2	11	2	Doncaster	5	13	9
11	6	14	Gillingham	7	11	9
6	5	10	Halifax	17	10	16
3	7	3	Hartlepool	10	12	13
14	3	16	Hereford	8	4	6
8	4	14	Lincoln	11	2	7
19	15	18	Maidstone	20	15	18
13	10	11	Northampton	15	6	13
9	6	12	Peterborough	3	3	3
2	1	6	Rochdale	4	6	4
18	14	18	Scarborough	19	14	17
1	7	1	Scunthorpe	1	11	2
7	7	7	Stockport	14	4	11
9	12	5	Torquay	10	9	10
4	8	4	Walsall	16	7	15
13	7	14	Wrexham	4	12	7
17	13	12	York	12	8	12

Example	Scunthorpe is best for Home Score-draws, and for Away Score-draws.

Doncaster is second best for Home Score-Draws and for all Home Draws.

TABLE SIX : DRAW PERFORMANCE RATINGS BY TEAMS

SCOTTISH PREMIER

HOME DRAWS   **AWAY DRAWS**

All Draws	No Score Draws	Score Draws	Teams	Score Draws	No Score Draws	All Draws
8	6	9	Aberdeen	1	8	3
9	9	6	Celtic	8	6	8
4	1	7	Dundee United	4	2	2
1	3	1	Dunfermline	3	6	4
3	7	2	Hearts	4	1	1
2	2	3	Hibernians	4	5	4
5	8	4	Motherwell	5	8	7
7	5	8	Rangers	2	4	3
6	6	6	St Johnstone	6	7	6
4	4	5	St Mirren	7	3	5

Example	Dunfermline is best for Home Score-draws and for all Home Draws.

Aberdeen is best for Away Score Draws and third best for all Away draws.

Hearts is best for Away No Score-draws and for all Away Draws.

USING TABLE SIX

You will have noticed that the Score-Draw Rating columns are placed next to the Teams on either side. This is deliberate because that is the rating which most people will look at first. Taking the Score-Draw rating of the Home and Away teams, comparing them, and using those matches in which the combined rating are the lowest, is the way to find the best pointers from this Table.

There will of course be occasions when the above does not produce the required number of selections without using matches where the combined values are quite high. This in itself may not deter some readers from using such matches. Others will prefer to adopt a different strategy in making their choices from the Table. Options include:

- Using those matches where either the Home or Away Team have very low ratings (e.g. 1 to 4) regardless of the other Teams rating;

- Using a combination of Score-Draw and No-Score Draw ratings and taking the matches with the lowest value;

- Using matches where all four values when added together, are the lowest. This means adding both the Score and No-Score Draw ratings, for both the Home and Away teams;

- Using the best indicators from the No Score Column only;

- Using the ALL DRAWS column, taking the best - i.e. the lowest unused indicators.

You may of course prefer some other approach in making up your total selections. The Sequence Tables published in daily papers about mid-week will give you some pointers to Home or Away Teams which are overdue a Score-Draw. These can be matched against the ratings given in the Table. Equally, Table Six can be used with other Tables. My preference is to use the Score-Draw ratings first, and then to make up any additional selections by using Tables 3, 2, 4, and 5 in that order, taking those matches which are well indicated in those Tables and have the lowest values in unused Table Six indicators, i.e. where the coupon number and match (Teams) line up. I rarely need to go beyond Table 3; you have the freedom to make your choice of approach in using Table Six with or without other Tables.

USING THE TABLES IN COMBINATIONS

In the previous pages, the possibilities of using the Tables individually or in various combinations to suit the readers choice, has been mentioned a few times. It is worth exploring the range of choices which basically spring from:

- Using any one of the Tables because it suits your needs;

- Using a combination of two or more Tables, which together meet your entry requirements.

Using any two Tables (and remembering that Tables 1 and 2 cannot effectively be used together because they have the same base) provides the following combinations:

Table 1 with Table 3, or 4, or 5, or 6 =   4 Combinations
Table 2 with Table 3, or 4, or 5, or 6 =   4 Combinations
Table 3 with Table 4, or 5, or 6 =   3 Combinations
Table 4 with Table 5 or 6 =   2 Combinations
Table 5 with Table 6 =   1 Combination

Taking any three Tables, and excluding those combinations in which Tables 1 and 2 are brought together, provides:

Tables: 1, 3, 4,   1, 3, 5,   1, 3, 6,   1, 4, 5,   1, 4, 6,   1, 5, 6   16
2, 3, 4,   2, 3, 5,   2, 3, 6,   2, 4, 5,   2, 4, 6,   2, 5, 6   Combinations
3, 4, 5,   3, 4, 6,   4, 5, 6,

For four Tables, with the same exclusion as above, the variations are:

Tables: 1, 3, 4, 5,   1, 3, 4, 6,   1, 3, 5, 6   9
1, 4, 5, 6,   2, 3, 4, 5,   2, 3, 4, 6   Combinations
2, 3, 5, 6,   2, 4, 5, 6,   3, 4, 5, 6

For five Tables (excluding combined Tables 1 and 2)   2

Tables: 1, 3, 4, 5, 6 and   2, 3, 4, 5, 6   2 Combinations

And of course for all six Tables, used perhaps separately to provide six or more separate entries on your coupon, there is only one "Combination" available.

In all therefore, you have 48 combinations available, one or more of which should prove helpful in the crucial task of selecting likely Score-Draws and putting you on the road to becoming a WINNER.

COMBINED TABLES : SOME EXAMPLES

Covering all the various combinations of Tables is neither practical nor necessary. Most readers will already have their preference, whether single or combined; some may find a few pointers helpful. I should make it clear that in these examples, the use of Tables is mostly straightforward i.e. based on the obvious "Best" indicators with a few variations here and there. An underlying purpose of the examples is to stimulate readers own thoughts. So if you read one or more of the given examples and think "I could do better than that with those Tables" that is fine.

To start with, take Tables One and Three.

Listing the top 29 numbers from Table One (i.e. from 15 down to 33, gives a good starting point.

Next mark off against these 29, all the Table Three indicators including those which appear more than once in that Table (e.g. No.19 appears twice and should be marked twice).

If you have done the above correctly, and you now sort out those numbers which appear twice or more in the two Tables, you will have 24 numbers; I list them here in numerical order;

1, 2, 5, 6, 8, 11, 12, 15, 16, 17, 18, 19,
23, 27, 28, 29, 30, 38, 39, 40, 42, 45, 47, 51

With 24 selections, you have a range of choices;

- 12 Pairs;
- 8 groups of 3; - 6 groups of 4;
- 4 groups of 6;
- 3 groups of 8

Possibilities for covering the above choices include:

Any 4 pairs from 12 pairs = 495 lines

Any 1 from 3 in each of 8 groups of 3 = 6561 lines = £6.56p on Zetters (Super Stake)

Any 2 groups of 8 from 3 groups = 3 sets of 16 numbers, to be covered by a perm of your choice.

Any 2 groups of 4 from 6 groups = 15 lines of 8 (not enough on their own to meet staking requirements, but groups can of course be varied many times)

Any 2 groups of 6 from 4 groups = 6 sets of 12 numbers to be covered by your chosen perm.

Two simple reminders are worth giving:

- If you want **less** than the total of numbers shown in these examples, take out those with either the lowest values or which appear towards the bottom of the Table(s) in question. If you want more numbers, try extending the choices from the combination you are using, or add numbers from another Table. And do not forget the many mentions of numbers 56 - 58 which have shown up so well in Score-Draw terms, since they were brought into use in 1985.

What if you want to combine Tables Two and Three?

Taking the top 4 from each of the five sections of Table **Two**, and matching these selections against **all** Table **Three** numbers (counted or marked as many times as they appear), provides a good basis for selections.

If you look for those numbers which appear 3 times, you will find 11 of them:

11, 15, 16, 28, 29, 39, 45, 47, 48, 49, 50

The above selections can easily be covered with a full cover perm of any 8 from 11 = 165 lines. On the very cheap pool (Zetters) you will need extra entries due to the minimum stake rule. Your 11 selections could become 14 by adding numbers 56 - 58. Full cover cost of any 8 from 14 would be:

Littlewoods: £30.00 (a bit expensive on this pool!)

Vernons: £8.58 (suitable for a small syndicate)

Zetters: £3.00 (ideal for a shared cost entry)

To extend the original 11 selections to 18, add in those numbers which appear twice; the result is:

2, 11, 12, 15, 16, 17, 19, 27, 28,
29, 39, 40 , 45, 47, 48, 49, 50, 51.

Choices in covering 18 selections exclude full cover because of the cost (£43.76 even on the cheapest pool at their super stake). Other, more sensible choices include 3 groups of 6, made into 3 entries of 12 matches which on Vernons (for example) would cost £4.24 using an "Any 8 from 12" approach. Varied sets of 9 pairs, each covered by "Any 4 pairs from 9 pairs" would cost £1.26 per entry on Littlewoods, and 13 pence (rounded) on Zetters using their super stake.

In discussing the Tables with friends and other football pools fanatics, I generally find that Tables Three and Four attract more attention than the rest. (If you are interested, you may like to know that Tables Six, Two, One and Five form the rest of the "Pecking Order").

Combining Tables Three and Four is a little more difficult than the examples already given. This because of the four columns in Table Three and the three in Table Four, plus the fact that various numbers appear more than once in different columns of both Tables. Effective comparison is therefore both complex and multi-varied, i.e. open to many approaches.

One way of bringing the Tables together as a combined basis of selection is:

- List the coupon numbers from the "Best" column of Table Three.

- Look for those numbers under "Coupon No." in Table Four and check which of them pair with another number from the same list in Col.2 of Table Four. An example would be 6 and 17, both of which are listed under "Best" in Table Three, and are linked in Table Four (Coupon No. plus Best Pair column). Nos. 15 and 17 are another example, as are 16 and 54.

- Do likewise with the 2nd Best Column in Table Three and 2nd Best Pair in Table Four. Repeat with the 3rd column from each Table.

Remember that, with Table Four, opposites are not necessarily equal. As an example, No.48 does **not** appear against Coupon No.22, but the latter **does** show up against Coupon No. 48, under 3rd Best pair(s). Bear this in mind when looking at the list below, which is my version of the above exercise given first in numerical order and then as pairs:

| 2, 3, 5, 6, 8, 11, 15, 16, 17, 19, 22, 23, 25, 27, 28, 28, | Given as 26 |
| 39, 40, 42, 43, 45, 46, 47, 48, 50, 54 | numbers |

2 + 16, 3 + 27, 5 + 29, 5 + 39, 6 + 17, 6 + 43, 8 + 15,	
11 + 28, 15 + 17, 16 + 23, 16 + 54, 17 + 50, 19 + 54,	Given as 24
22 + 48, 23 + 25, 23 + 28, 27 + 28, 28 + 48, 37 + 45,	Pairs
40 + 42, 42 + 49, 45 + 48, 46 + 49, 47 + 54.	

If you choose to take either the above numbers (or pairs) as the basis of your entry, the "Groups" approach is probably best, i.e. making entries of 12 or 15 or whatever, by combining groups of 3 or 4 to make up individual entries of your chosen perm.

Examples given so far, have dealt with Tables where indicators are fixed, i.e. they stand throughout the entire season. Tables Five and Six are in a different category, i.e. their indicators change from week to week. When combining one of these variable Tables with any of the fixed-indicator Tables, it is therefore best to give dominance to Table Five or Six, rather than to regard the combination as equally balanced, i.e. the same weight for both Tables. The exception to this is of course a combination of Tables Five and Six, where both are in the variable category.

It is fairly easy to use Table Six as a way of comparing Score-Draw performance for each of the teams making up a match in any week. And since the best indicators are the matches where the combined Score-Draw values are lowest, it does not take long to find the best selections. Comparing these with Table Five Column A (across) for the given week can also be done easily. You will probably need to use Column B (across) for the same week, on most occasions. Unused selections from Table Five can be brought in if your required total is not met. If you prefer Table Six, the notes on using that Table show alternative methods of finding extra selections.

When using Table Six in combination with other Tables (including Table Five), it is best to treat the identified matches as the coupon numbers against which they appear. An example of easy comparison is to combine Table Two and Six, since both are Divisional/Group based when looked at as coupon numbers. It will not always be the case that Division 1 coincides exactly with Group 1 in Table Two, but in many weeks this will be the case. In any event, the conversion of Table Six matches into numbers makes comparison an easy task.

Table Five with its changing weekly numbers can be used with Tables 1 or 2 (but not effectively with **both**) and of course with any other combination from the remaining Tables.

COMBINED TABLES:
A FEW FINAL THOUGHTS

Examples on previous pages have concentrated on combinations of 2 tables. It is also true that not all such combinations were explored. As mentioned earlier, the purpose of these examples is to stimulate your own thoughts, rather than to fill up pages with all of the various combinations possible with 6 tables. The examples should be enough for most people, either on their own, or as a pointer to forming and using combinations of their choice.

It is also worth making the point again that all the tables can be used on their own. For the many readers who see that as the easiest and most sensible way of getting the best from the Tables, let me say clearly that I imply no specific benefit in using combinations; I point to them because for some readers, such usage will be attractive.

The point of all this is that it is your choice which matters. You will recall that the purpose of the tables is to help you put your selection process on a sound basis. If your preference is to continue spending your stake money on entries based purely on luck or random selections, then that is your right. Now that you can see the patterns/trends evident in actual results, you may want to use one or more tables in the ways already discussed or in ways of your own. And you can of course include a "Luck-based" or random entry on your coupon - if you want to do so - in addition to Tables - based entries. This is easily possible on the lower cost pools.

OTHER METHODS OF DRAW SELECTION

"The Tables are really useful; a real aid to Score Draw selection".

"The Tables are about as useful as a knapsack of sand on a trek across the Sahara".

You may share one or other of the above views, or perhaps something in between. In my experience, the great majority of opinions about the Tables are closer to the first comment than to the second. The latter tends to come from people stubbornly locked in to using a pet method of their own, be it totally random selections, the same set of teams or numbers every week, or some theory about recent form or whatever. I do not ridicule such approaches; if people are happy with them, well that's their business. To play Devil's Advocate, isn't it true that we frequently hear about a big win for someone whose entry is based on house numbers, shoe sizes, childrens ages or something similar? The answer is of course, yes we do, but not as frequently as we think it happens and more importantly, we forget that for every such winner, there are millions of losers.

Having said all that, there is scope for considering other methods of selecting potential Score-Draws. I cannot write about all of them because (A) I don't **know** all of them and (B) many are variations on a theme so to speak. What I can do is to briefly describe some of these methods. If your favourite approach is not among those I mention, then my apologies (but do write and tell me about it if you wish!)

In the days **before** the introduction of Score-Draws, when every draw had equal value, the sporting press regularly displayed advertisements for pet systems and the like, all promising sure-fire 1st Dividend wins, or 8 draws guaranteed or something similar. There is a lot less of that sort of thing these days, and most of what is offered often consists of permutation based approaches.

The popular press in their regular weekly articles (on the pools pages about mid-week) tend to also concentrate on perms rather than on selection approaches. This is a pity because they have such a wealth of information available and could probably use that as the basis of some imaginative ideas to put before the public. For my part, let me describe some methods; who knows, one or more of them may appeal to you.

OTHER METHODS OF DRAW SELECTION CONTINUED

In the above heading the word "Score" has been dropped because in widening the focus on methods of selection, it is virtually impossible to avoid approaches in which the type of drawn result is not of primary interest. In many such approaches, the focus is on a draw; the majority of the latter type results are Score-Draws. It is therefore fair and reasonable to include these approaches as pointers to selections.

Sequence tables in daily papers have already been mentioned a few times. I do not propose to dwell upon that approach except to say that my use of such tables is firmly based on linkages i.e. I use them only when the matches they indicate are **also** indicated by one or more of the Tables in previous pages. I would never rely on sequences alone even if they gave sufficient matches for my entry. But that of course is a purely personal view.

What about Pontoon Tables? It is common to see such Tables in the tabloid press, usually covering the past 4 weeks and showing the goals scored by each team (per week) over that period. Many years ago, they showed 6 weeks goals; it is my personal belief that this was more useful. Readers who follow or use Pontoon Table figures can of course easily set up their own records for any number of weeks they choose, but I believe that 6 is about right. About right for what, you may ask? The pointer to a potential draw result lies in the goals scored figures.. Where both teams in a match show a goals figure **of 2 or less** over the 4 week period (preferably 6 weeks), then mark those on a spare or old coupon, with the total used as markers. If you need 16 selections, take those with the lowest totals. Should more matches be needed than are indicated, take those with the combined lowest totals from unused games. If too many indications are thrown up, take out those with a majority of 2s in their combined 4 (or 6) week record.

Variations on this approach are possible. For some people, it is enough if the Home Team qualifies. This will of course bring out more selections. Others may prefer to link Table Six to Pontoon Table usage, taking those matches where either one or both teams qualify in both Tables. Other Tables can also be used in link with Pontoon Tables, but for some readers, the latter-on their own - may be enough to give a sensible basis to their selections.

OTHER METHODS OF DRAW
SELECTION CONTINUED

League position (of individual teams) is of great interest to some pools enthusiasts. Again, this is information freely available in the press. And every team must be somewhere in the league, moving up or down according to their fortunes on the field.

What to look for? Start with teams playing at home; identify those who are in the top 5 of their league. Do likewise for each Division. Next, look at teams playing away and identify those in the bottom 5 of their league and repeat this for all Divisions. In most weeks this will give enough indicators, i.e. the matches where one or both teams qualify under the above guidelines. For some purists, the preference will be for matches where both teams qualify, but this is too restrictive in most weeks. For those who like the original approach, extra selections can be found by extending the rule about league position to 6 instead of 5, but I would not recommend going beyond this.

Goal averages provide another basis for selecting potential draws. With this approach, some variations are also possible. First, for those who are not familiar with League Tables, they usually show - for each team - the number of matches played, won, drawn and lost, with "For" and "Against" figures, all given separately for Home and Away performances. It is the "For" and "Against" columns which are of interest, particularly the "For" figure of the Home Team and the "Against" figure for the Away Team. In effect, these figures represent the performance values of the two teams. The first thing to do is to add the values together for each team in each match of your choice (or for all matches if you have the time and the inclination). If you need - for example - 18 matches, take the 18 with the lowest combined totals. Here is an example:

Match	Home	For	Against	Away	For	Against	Total
A	Team 1	13	10	Team 2	7	15	= 28
B	Team 3	11	4	Team 4	8	6	= 17
C	Team 5	7	5	Team 6	4	7	= 14
D	Team 7	10	11	Team 8	5	10	= 20
E	Team 8	9	9	Team 9	8	6	= 15
F	Team 10	16	7	Team 11	5	13	= 29

Clearly in the above example, Matches C and E are the lowest in total and would be the selections from this batch.

The method just described tends to single out matches where low scoring Home teams meet Away teams who are fairly strong in defence. Some people will see this as a pointer to likely Away wins. But in theory at least, the Home team has the advantage of being at home **and** will certainly be trying not to lose. Therefore, the result is just as likely to be a draw.

I mentioned earlier that variations are possible with a method based on goal average. Strictly speaking, the latter should be goals divided by matches played (e.g. a "For" figure of 26 in 13 matches played equals an average of 2). Since averages depend on this combination, the actual "For" figure - or "Against" figure - can be used for comparison purposes. Some people prefer to take all four figures, i.e. the For/Against figures for both Home **and** Away teams, add the lot together and use the lowest overall totals as the best indicators.

Another variation is to use the "For" columns only, for both teams, concentrating on the difference between the figures. The lower the difference, the better the draw potential according to this theory, since the scoring ability of each team in their respective Home and Away roles, is the key issue.

Other variations are possible, and some of them are used by people with a fixed preference for particular approaches, and - usually - lots of time. As an example, some enthusiasts (I hesitate in using the word fanatics since I might justifiably be so labelled for various reasons) actually work out the differences in plus and minus terms, between the For and Against figures for both Home and Away teams separately. So a 15 (For) and 12 (Against) for the Home team would result in + 3 and a 12 for and 15 against for the Away team would result in - 3. One cancels the other out (+ 3 and - 3 = 0) so the "Value" for that particular match would be NIL. Again the lowest values would be the chosen selections. But doing this for all matches on the coupon takes time.

The above variations on the goal average theme may raise your interest in this approach and perhaps give rise to your own ideas on how to use the figures. If you want to test any of the above theories - or one of your own - try tracking back on actual results compared with the For and Against columns of each team. For myself, I will say only that the principle of using matches where both teams have low averages has some appeal, but not enough to make me want to spend a lot of time in calculations etc. You may of course disagree.

All the approaches described so far - and the six Tables - depend on past results and their interpretation. One theory about past results focuses on the outcome of matches played **prior** to the week in which the particular team appears on the pools coupon. The idea expressed in its simplest form, is that a draw is likely when previous results fall into particular patterns. This means record-keeping on a rather extensive scale, which may appeal to people with plenty of time and/or access to a computer. The idea of keeping records is enough to put some people off, but the theory is worth exploring at least in outline.

One match can - obviously - have 3 possible results, - i.e. win, lose or draw; in a shortened form, this becomes W, L, D. For each teams **previous** match, two sets of W, L, D are possible since they must have either won, lost or drawn. For the previous 2 matches of each team, 9 results per team are possible i.e. 3 x 3 or

WW	WL	WD	Home	WW	WL	WD	Away
LL	LW	LD	Teams	LL	LW	LD	Teams
DW	DL	DD	2 previous	DW	DL	DD	2 previous

For 3 previous games there are 27 possible combinations per team i.e. 3 x 3 x 3. I show below one set of 27 results which of course applies to both teams separately.

WWW	WLW	WDW	LLL	LWW	LDW	DDD	DLL	DWD
WWL	WLL	WDL	LLW	LWL	LDL	DDW	DLW	DWL
WWD	WLD	WDD	LLD	LWD	LDD	DDL	DLD	DWW

When a draw occurs (after one; two or three games) it must follow one of the above combinations. The theory is that records over time are likely to point to draws following particular combinations. This is fine as theory, but difficult and time consuming since 9 combinations are needed just for one previous result per team (3 x 3). For two previous results, 81 combinations are needed (9 x 9). And for 3 prior results, 729 combinations are required (27 x 27), which is why I refer above to time and to computer usage. Daunting though it may be, I believe the approach has merit and for those capable of using it at the 2 or 3 prior games level, it could be rewarding. For the record, I have not tried it. I would like to hear from those who have.

All the popular dailies have pools "Experts". Some of the specialist sporting pages give a summary table of experts opinions on the given weeks matches results, i.e. their forecasts, usually shown under 1 (win) 1 1/2 (Away win) 2 (No Score Draw) or X (Draw). Typically, you will find 10 or perhaps 20 experts opinions summarised for each match, e.g.

Experts	1(W)	2 (Away Win)	X (Draw)	Likely Result
10	6	3	1	1 or 2
20	9	4	7	1 or X

It is a fairly simple task to go down the list of summarised views and look for those matches where:

- A draw is clearly indicated by the majority "Votes",

- A draw or away result (X or 1 1/2) is the dominant view.

- A draw or home win (X or 1) is in the majority.

Does this method of selection have any merit? The answer must be yes if you consider that it is easy to do, your chosen batch of matches have at least the same chances as those picked at random, and you are relying on expert opinion. If on the other hand, you track back on these experts, you may find their actual results less than encouraging. And when did you last read of one of them finding 8 draws in a week? This is not criticism as such. Any or all of those experts would be delighted with success and probably try hard to make correct predictions. Their lack of success goes to show how difficult it is to correctly forecast enough draws to produce a dividend. But then if it was easy, there would be no high dividends. And when the experts are right about a particular match, that is often a "Form" draw, i.e. a game which virtually everyone expected to end up with an even result, rather like the hot favourite in a horse racing event.

Apart from their opinions on expected results, experts tend to confine their "Help" to articles about the virtues of various permutations. I would like to see them using the vast amount and variety of information available to them; to form, test out, and make public some imaginative approaches to selecting potential draws, particularly Score-Draws. But perms are important and the next section deals with that aspect of pools entries.

PERMUTATIONS

The vast majority of the millions of pools entries fall into one of 5 categories:

1. **Full Cover Perms** e.g. "Any 8 from 11 = 165 lines", or "Perm any 4 from (5, 6, 7, 8 or whatever) with any 4 from (5, 6, 7 etc)". In the case of 6 selections, this would be: "Perm any 4 from 6 with any 4 from 6 = 15 x 15 = 225 lines".

The full cover Table at the start of this book tells you the total of lines required for full cover perms. Their advantage is obvious; every draw counts on every line of the perm, in which it occurs. The disadvantage is the cost which rises rapidly as the number of selections increase. Nonetheless, they remain a firm favourite with many people because of the watertight guarantees they provide. Probably the most popular full cover entry is the good old "Any 8 from 10 = 45 lines". I shall shortly be exploring some ways of retaining full cover guarantee, combined with some variations on the standard entry for full cover perms.

2. **Conditional Guarantee Perms**, e.g. the type which guarantees that if your selections contain a given number of draws, then one of your entry lines must bring 7 or 8 of them together. There are, equally, very strong opinions as to their value. Some pundits abhor them as little more than a waste of money. Others extol their virtues particularly the ability to cover a number of matches at well below the full cover cost, thus either reducing expense or enabling the individual to make multiple entries for the same cost as one full cover entry. Where do I stand on this division of opinion? Firmly on both sides; that is not fence-sitting since I have good reason for my view. I detest those perms which guarantee 7 on a line if 8 or 9 or whatever, are correct in my selections. On the other hand, I quite like **some** of the conditional guarantee perms which quite clearly tell me that I will have 8 correct on one line if there are 9 (or whatever) correct in my

total selections. I underlined some because even with this clear cut guarantee, some of these perms are more expensive that they need be, and others lack any secondary guarantees, such as "8 will guarantee 7" and "7 will guarantee either one line with all 7, or multiple lines with 6 correct". Again, I shall say more about this method of entry later.

3. **Block Perms:** This type of entry is perhaps less popular now than in the 1950's/1960's, but is still a favoured entry method for many people. Essentially, it consists of 2 or more "Blocks" or sets of lines, with any line from one block being permed with any line from another (or any 2 lines from one with any 2 from the other etc: many variations are possible with block entries).

Here is a simple example: (I am using the top twenty selections from Table One to illustrate the Block Entry method).

Coupon No.											Notes
2											In this example, only the No's covered are shown. On a real coupon there would of course be all the other coupon No's.
6											
8											
10					Block A						
11											
12											
13											
15											
16											
17											Matches 17 and 45 are marked only once because the "Example Investor" is doubtful about their chances.
19											
21											
23											
27											
28	Block B										
29											
30											
39											
40											
45											

Perm any line from Block A with any line from Block B = 7 x 7 = 49 lines at 1p = 49p staked.

The above is an **EXAMPLE ONLY, NOT** a recommended entry!

There are many ways of exploiting BLOCKS; I shall give some examples later.

4. **Pairs:** This method of entry in which matches are paired up in twos (not necessarily consecutive) remains popular and in my view justifiably so. It can be relatively cheap, it is easy to enter on coupons, it allows for wide coverage which would cost must more on a full cover basis, and since the average Score-Draws per week is 10, there must equally be an average of 5 pairs per week over time. The disadvantages? Well the great problem is of course that you need 4 pairs correct (unless there are fewer than 8 draws) to win a 1st Dividend, and which matches do you pair together? The first of those points is a fact of life, and the second point may be answered by reference to Table Four.

The same group or total of selections can of course be paired in many ways. Here is an example using the top 4 from Group 1 of Table Two, with the top 3 from each of the other Groups, i.e. 16 selections in all. Again, only the coupon numbers used are shown.

Coupon No.	A	B	C	
2				
10				
11				
12				
15				
16				
19				
28				
29				
30				
39				
40				
45				
48				
50				
51				

Perm any 4 pairs from 8 pairs in each of blocks A, B and C = 70 x 3 = 210 lines.

The above is a very simple example; more will be said about Pairs later. Note that in each Block (A, B, C) each match number appears only once. Success is dependent on 4 paired numbers producing a Score-Draw. And if you have the time and the money, extra blocks could be entered up to your maximum stake. In many forms of paired entries the pairs are given in brackets on the same line of the entry.

5. **Single Lines**: Not a method I would recommend to anyone, but some diehards still prefer it. In brief, it consists of writing lines of 8 selections on the coupon, up to whatever maximum stake is being used. Not popular with pools firms either; the availability of full cover and other perms - which can be entered on coupons quite easily - makes the need for single line entries out of date. I shall not be wasting time discussing them.

Older readers will remember that years ago, the uses and disadvantages of "Guarantee Blocks" were widely publicised. Before moving on to examples of actual entries using various permutations, I want to show some of these guarantee blocks and explain how they may be used with a little imagination. What does the term "Guarantee Block" mean? In short, it is a way of covering a group of matches in such a way as to ensure that a given number of correct results will produce a line with a guaranteed minimum of those results in it. As an example, let us assume that you want to cover 5 matches so as to guarantee that if 3 are correct (i.e. Score-Draws), at least 2 will come together on one line. We already know from the Full Cover Table that any 2 or any 3 from 5 means 10 lines. To guarantee 2 if 3 are correct in 5, takes only 4 lines:

Match No.	Block 1			
1	X			
2	X			
3		X	X	
4		X		X
5			X	X

If any 3 are correct, 2 of them must appear again on one of the four lines shown.

Staying with the basic guarantee of 2 correct on one line if 3 are correct in the total of selections, here are the lines needed to cover various numbers of matches:

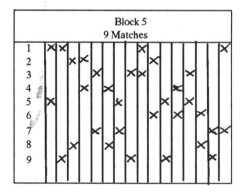

Block 2 6 Matches	Block 3 7 Matches	Block 4 8 Matches
Any 3 correct in the 6 selections means that 2 of them must be on one of the 6 lines shown.	As aside, but 9 lines are needed.	As aside, but 12 columns needed.

Block 5
9 Matches

Same guarantee, but 16 columns needed.

Moving on to 3 correct on a line if 4 are correct in the total of selections:

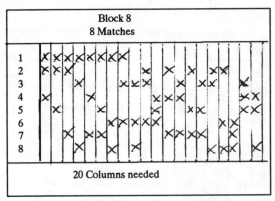

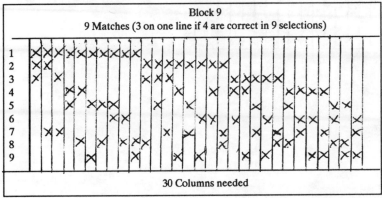

And finally, in those few examples of Guarantee Blocks, we move on to 4 correct on one line if a given number are correct in the total of selections.

Below are the blocks covering 6, 7, 8 and 9 matches, each with a guarantee that if 5 are correct in the total of matches in the block, 4 must come together on one line.

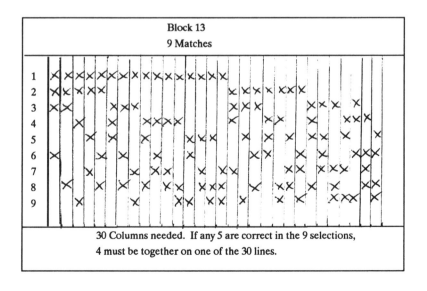

Block 10	Block 11	Block 12
6 Matches	7 Matches	8 Matches
3 Columns needed	7 Columns needed	14 Columns needed

Block 13

9 Matches

30 Columns needed. If any 5 are correct in the 9 selections, 4 must be together on one of the 30 lines.

Readers familiar with these blocks will know that the above is only a sample. Anyone who wants a block covering 10 or more matches with various guarantees, should write to their pools firm, being very precise about their requirements, e.g. "A block covering 11 matches with a guarantee that if 5 are correct in the 11, 4 must come together on one line."

The point I want to make about such Blocks is that they are usually seen (and used) as covering single matches or numbers. They can of course be used to cover pairs or groups; for example, 7 groups of 3 matches each can be linked or made into 7 entries of 12 matches / numbers with the certainty that 4 of the best 5 groups must come together. More on this approach later.

PERMUTATIONS AND ACTUAL ENTRIES

My philosophy about "Doing the Pools" is simple: Make every entry count, i.e. sound selections and sensible permutations. So even if you pick your matches/numbers at random or stick rigidly to the same set of selections every week, do at least use a good perm to cover them.

Imagine having every draw on the coupon in your perm and ending up with a 4th Dividend. This sort of thing is far from impossible. An acquaintance of mine used - for many years - a perm covering 16 selections which guaranteed that if 9 were correct in the 16, he would have at least 7 on one line of his entry. In one unforgettable week, there were 11 draws on the coupon, and he had them all in his 16 matches. But checking - and double-checking - showed that nowhere did he have 8 on a line. He perhaps naturally assumed that if 9 guaranteed 7, then 10 might guarantee 8 and 11 were surely bound to do so. That was to put it mildly, a mistaken assumption. He got his guaranteed 7, with the 8th match being a home win, and duly received a small sum from the pools company.

The moral in the above tale is - or should be - very clear. Never, never, never use permutations which do not make quite clear how many selections must be correct to produce a line of 8 draws. If full cover perms do not meet your needs or are too costly, then by all means fall back on conditional guarantee entries but only those in which the outcome will be 8 on a line if a given number are correct in your total selections. And even then, shop around; the same guarantee for the same number of matches may be available elsewhere at a lower cost. Most of the tabloid papers will send you copies of their perms at no cost other than a stamped addressed envelope. Comparison is often worthwhile, i.e. you will find that some plans covering the same number of matches, are cheaper than others.

In the following pages, I give examples of entries covering from 12 matches up to virtually the whole coupon. In these examples, the Tables are used as the basis for selections. They are of course only examples. Use them if you wish, but you may prefer to adapt one or more of them to your needs, or to go your own way so to speak. Either way, what matters is that your entry is sound and that you do all you can to reduce the odds against you. And when the magic high dividend cheque comes through your letter box, do write and let me know, particularly if the Tables or other information has helped in your achievement.

NOTES ON ENTRIES

The pages which follow illustrate examples of actual entries, with costs shown for illustrative purposes only, i.e. the actual cost will depend on which coupon you use and whether you make one entry or many. At the time of writing, the cost per line on the four pools firms coupon is:

> Littlewoods - 1p per line
> Vernons - 2/7p per line
> Zetters - 1/15p per line, or 1/10p Super Stake
> Brittens - 1/25p per line

(Note: These costs may change; check your coupon).

There is - as you can see - a fair range of variety available, with dividends being paid in proportion to the stake. A minimum stake applies on all pools; where an example entry in the following pages is at a lower cost than the minimum, you will need to allow for this if using the example shown, by making one or more additional entries.

In the examples, firm instructions are written in full. On actual coupons you will find boxes in which to mark your Full Cover perms or any one of a range of listed newspaper plans. You will also find a space in which to enter any unlisted plan you may want to use. If in doubt about old plans, check with the pools company first, to ensure that it is acceptable.

Do remember that examples quoted in the following pages are only examples. For any given number of selections, there will be many ways of entering them on your coupon, using either Full Cover, conditional guarantee perms, a "Block" type entry perhaps using one or more of the blocks already given in this book, or paired selections or whatever. Whether your selections come from the Tables or not, do make the most of your entry.

COVERING 12 SELECTIONS

Perm any 8 from 12 = 495 lines @ 1p = £4.95 staked

Perm 8 from 12 out of any 4 columns of 3 from 5 columns
= 495 x 5 = 2475 lines @ 1/10p = £2.47 staked

On Full Cover, 8 from 12 costs 495 lines, which is within scope for most people, on any pool.

With Full Cover, every draw counts; if you get 8 correct in your 12 selections - taken perhaps from Table 2 or Table 3 - you must have a 1st Dividend line of 24 points.

This is the only example where a simple Full Cover entry is shown. For other selection totals, e.g. 13, or 14 or whatever, refer to the Permutation Table and adjust your entry, instructions and cost accordingly.

The second example shown aside, extends to 15 matches entered as groups of 12, and is the type of entry which is ideal for lower cost pools. It could of course be extended to cover more selections at a higher cost.

ENTRIES OF 12 SELECTIONS

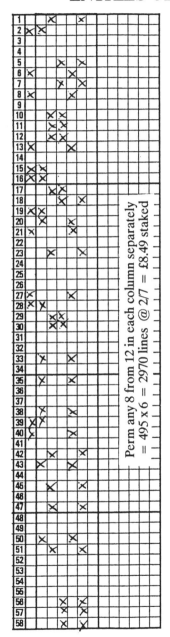

Perm any 8 from 12 in each column separately @ 2/7 = £8.49 staked = 495 x 6 = 2970 lines

In this Example, Block 1 (shown earlier) is used to combine 6 groups of 6 selections into 6 entries of 12 each. 2 of the best 3 groups must combine in one of the columns. If in any column of 12, you have 8 Score-Draws, you must win a 1st Dividend. Tables 1, 2, or 3 would be ideal sources of so many selections, i.e. 36 in all.

The cost would of course vary according to which pool you are using:

Vernons: As shown

Littlewoods: £29.70

Zetters: £2.97 (Super Stake)

Brittens: £1.19

ENTRIES OF 13 SELECTIONS

Perm any 4 from 6 in 1st column with any 4 from 7 in 2nd column = 15 x 35 = 525 lines @ 1p = £5.25 staked

Perm any 3 from 5 in first column with any 5 from 8 in second column = 10 x 56 = 560 lines @ 1/10p = 56 pence staked

Full Cover for 8 from 13 needs 1287 lines, which on cheaper pools is easily affordable.

The 2 examples, aside illustrate some cheaper variations.

1st Example Costs:

Littlewoods - As shown

Vernons - £1.50

Zetters - 52p (Super Stake)

Brittens - 21p

2nd Example Costs:

*Zetters - As shown
(Super Stake)*

Littlewoods - £5.60

Vernons - £1.60

Brittens - 23p (rounded)

ENTRIES OF 14 SELECTIONS

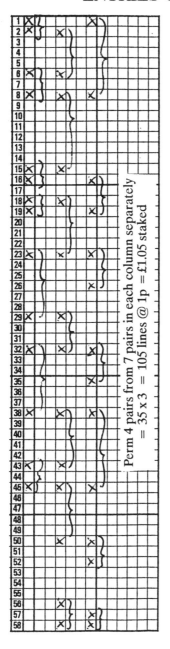

Perm 4 pairs from 7 pairs in each column separately = 35 x 3 = 105 lines @ 1p = £1.05 staked

To cover any 8 from 14 requires 3003 lines.

*Shown aside is an example of simple pairing of 14 selections. Multiple entries of this type are within reasonable cost limits, but do remember that you need 4 correct **pairs** on one line to get that elusive 1st Dividend. Table Four may be a useful source for entries based on pairs.*

Extensions are easily possible, e.g. 28 selections = 4 groups of 7. Any 2 groups from 4 groups = 6 entries of 14, each split into 7 pairs.

With the same instructions as aside but with 6 columns instead of 3, the cost becomes: 35 x 6 = 210 lines

Littlewoods - 2.10

Vernons - 60p

Zetters - 21p (Super Stake)

Brittens - 9p (Rounded)

On Zetters/Brittens, you will need extra entries to meet minimum stake requirements.

103

ENTRIES OF 14 SELECTIONS

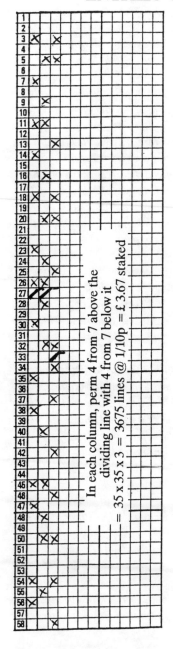

Entries of this type can be expensive. Careful selection, clear division of the groups of 7, and (perhaps) using the matches you are reasonably sure about, twice or 3 times are good guidelines. (In the example, 10 no's are marked twice).

For a simpler - and cheaper - entry, pick 14 selections, split them into 2 groups of 7 - using 2 coupon columns if necessary - and write:

"Perm 4 from 7 in each Group" (or column)

= 35 x 35 = 1225 lines

Cost:

Littlewoods - £12.25

Vernons - £3.50

Zetters - £1.22 (Super Stake)

Brittens - 49p

ENTRIES OF 14 SELECTIONS

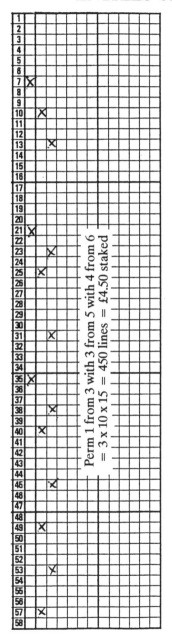

Aside is an example of mixed groups of numbers. Success depends on each group providing the required number of correct results. Other combinations are possible, such as 2 groups of 5 and 1 of 4, or 1 group of 6 and 2 of 4.

Using the 2nd set above:

Any 4 from 6 with any 2 from each of 2 groups of 4 =

15 x 6 x 6 = 540 lines

Cost:

Littlewoods - £5.40

Vernons - £1.54

Zetters - 54p (Super Stake)

Brittens - 22p

On lower cost pools, multiple entries are easily possible, and can be achieved by extending your total of selections to 21. Do make sure that each entry however it is made up, contains 14 selections.

ENTRIES OF 15 SELECTIONS

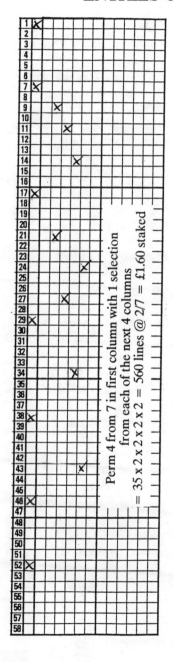

Perm 4 from 7 in first column with 1 selection
from each of the next 4 columns
= 35 x 2 x 2 x 2 x 2 = 560 lines @ 2/7 = £1.60 staked

6435 lines are needed to fully cover any 8 from 15 selections. The example aside is much cheaper, costing:

Vernons - as shown

Littlewoods - £5.60

Zetters - 56p (Super Stake)

Brittens - 23p (Rounded)

ENTRIES OF 15 SELECTIONS

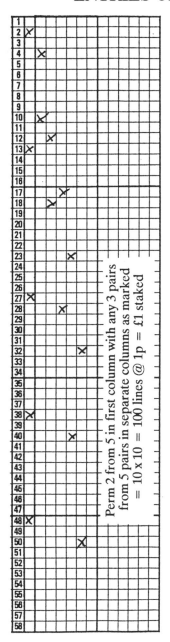

Perm 2 from 5 in first column with any 3 pairs
from 5 pairs in separate columns as marked
= 10 x 10 = 100 lines @ 1p = £1 staked

If you like to invest in paired results, an entry of this type can be very cheap, but does depend on getting both parts of the perm right, i.e. 3 correct in your 1st 5 matches and 3 correct pairs out of 5.
Equally, the low cost enables a wider spread of selections for multiple entry purposes.

Tables 3 and 4 might suit your purposes with this type of entry.

ENTRIES OF 15 SELECTIONS

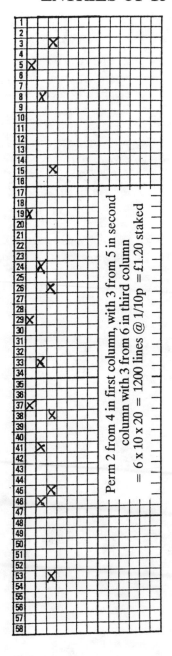

Perm 2 from 4 in first column, with 3 from 5 in second column with 3 from 6 in third column = 6 x 10 x 20 = 1200 lines @ 1/10p = £1.20 staked

An example of mixed groups (4 with 5 with 6) at a reasonable cost, and capable of variation or extension, notably on lower cost pools. The example shown costs:

Zetters - as shown (Super Stake)

Littlewoods - £12.00

Vernons - £3.43

Brittens - 48p

ENTRIES OF 15 SELECTIONS

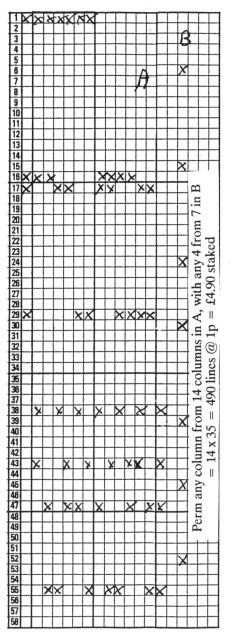

This example illustrates the use of Blocks to cover one part of a perm, with the other part being a straight 4 from 7.

Note that the 14 columns block covering 8 matches ensures that if 5 are correct in the 8, then 4 must be together on one line. If this is the case and you have 4 correct in your other 7 selections, you have your 1st Dividend line.

ENTRIES OF 16 SELECTIONS

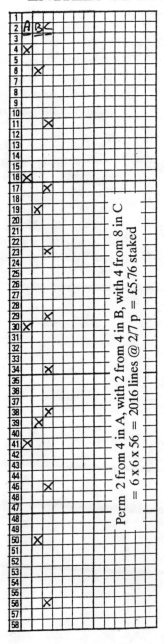

8 from 16 on Full Cover requires 12870 lines. A mixed group approach as aside may be the answer to a need for lower costs. Again, careful selection, plus equal care in making up your groups, is good advice, i.e. your "Strong" selections should be in the groups of 4. Cost:

Vernons - as shown

Littlewoods - £20.16

Zetters - £2.02 (Rounded) (Super Stake)

Brittens - 81p

ENTRIES OF 16 SELECTIONS

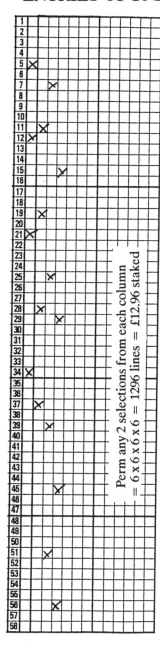

Perm any 2 selections from each column
= 6 x 6 x 6 x 6 = 1296 lines = £12.96 staked

A very simple way of dealing with 16 selections - success depends on getting 2 correct in each column of 4. The cost:

Littlewoods - as shown

Vernons - £3.70

Zetters - £1.30 (Super Stake)

Brittens - 52p

On the lower cost pools, extension to multiple entries is quite feasible e.g. by adding another column of 4 matches, making 5 columns in all. Write "Perm any 2 from 4 from any 4 columns of 5 columns" = 1296 x 5 = 6580 lines. Cost:

Zetters - £6.48 (Super Stake)

Brittens - £2.59

ENTRIES OF 16 SELECTIONS

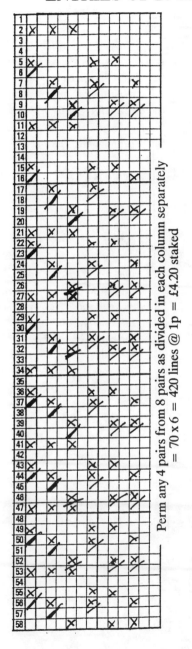

Perm any 4 pairs from 8 pairs as divided in each column separately = 70 x 6 = 420 lines @ 1p = £4.20 staked

For a cheap entry with wide cover, the Example aside may appeal to those who look to Table 4 for selections.

Do make sure your pairs are clearly separated. The astute perm expert will realise that in the 32 matches covered, each consecutive group of 4 selections is paired into 6 sets of 2. But of course you still need 4 successful pairs in ONE column, to win the magic 1st Dividend.

Cost:

Littlewoods - As shown

Vernons - £1.20

Zetters - 42p (Super Stake)

Brittens - 17p

On the lower cost pools, extension of this pairs approach is easily possible within reasonable cost.

ENTRIES OF 16 SELECTIONS

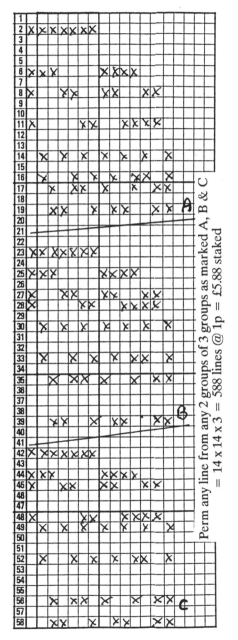

This example shows how 24 matches can be covered with the Block approach. Each Block (A,B,C) ensures that if 5 are correct in the 8 matches covered, then 4 must come together on 1 line of the block. If this happens in any 2 blocks, you have your 1st Dividend.

Cost:

Littlewoods - As shown
Vernons - £1.68
Zetters - 59p (Super Stake)
Brittens - 24p

Maximum extension of this approach is possible with 56 matches in 7 groups of 8, each covered by the Block layout as aside. Taking any 2 groups from 7 groups = 21 combinations of 14 x 14 or 4116 lines. Costly on

Littlewoods at £41.16, and Vernons at £11.76, but Zetters - £4.12 (Super Stake) Brittens - £1.65

NOTE that the groups as shown in the example could just as easily be spread down the coupon and set out side by side rather than as given. All Pools firms supply continuation sheets if needed.

Perm any line from any 2 groups of 3 groups as marked A, B & C
= 14 x 14 x 3 = 588 lines @ 1p = £5.88 staked

ENTRIES OF 17 SELECTIONS

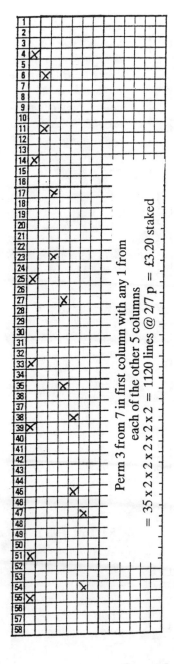

At 24310 lines, full cover for 17 matches is probably too expensive for most people. Even on the cheapest pool (Brittens) the cost is £9.72.

The example entry aside reduces the cost to a more reasonable level, and is of course capable of variation. For example, 5 matches in one column followed by 6 sets of 2, and taking any 2 from the column of 5 with any 1 from each of the 6 other columns (of 2) results in 10 x 2 x 2 x 2 x 2 x 2 x 2 = 640 lines.

Costs of the Example aside:

Vernons - As shown

Littlewoods - £11.20

Zetters - £1.12 (Super Stake)

Brittens - 45p (rounded)

ENTRIES OF 17 SELECTIONS

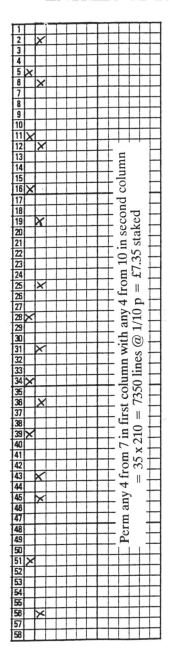

Perm any 4 from 7 in first column with any 4 from 10 in second column
= 35 x 210 = 7350 lines @ 1/10 p = £7.35 staked

Splitting your 17 selections into more manageable groups may be the answer for you. An obvious split is a group of 8 with a group of 9, taking any 4 from each group (70 x 126 = 8820 lines).

The example aside is slightly less expensive at 7350 lines. But with 7 selections in one column and 10 in the other, it is important to handle your split of selections carefully, i.e. put your best 7 together on one line, because you need 4 of them to be successful, combined with 4 others from the group of 10. Costs are:

*Zetters - as shown
(Super Stake)*

Littlewoods - £73.50

Vernons - £21.00

Brittens - £2.94

ENTRIES OF 17 SELECTIONS

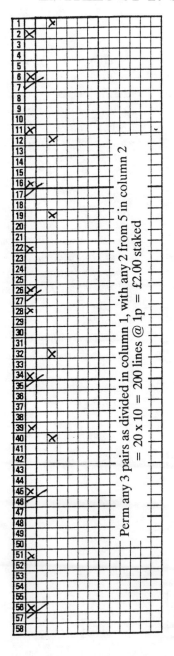

Perm any 3 pairs as divided in column 1, with any 2 from 5 in column 2 = 20 x 10 = 200 lines @ 1p = £2.00 staked

For those who like entries based on or including paired selections, the example aside may be useful. Cost is low and variation is possible in the number of matches used as pairs, e.g. any 2 pairs from 5 pairs with any 4 from the remaining 7, needs 350 lines (10 x 35).

The low cost of this example (aside) means that multiple entries are feasible, and will in any case be needed on low cost pools to meet minimum stake requirements.

Costs:

Littlewoods - as shown

Vernons - 57p

Zetters - 20p (Super Stake)

Brittens - 8p

ENTRIES OF 17 SELECTIONS

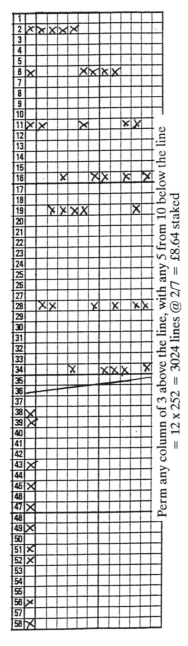

Perm any column of 3 above the line, with any 5 from 10 below the line
= 12 x 252 = 3024 lines @ 2/7 = £8.64 staked

This example shows how a block of 7 matches, (covered so that if 4 are correct in the 7, then 3 must appear in one of the 12 columns) can be combined with full cover for the remaining matches. Reference back to the blocks shown earlier will make the possibilities evident with this type of approach, e.g. 8 selections covered by a block of 14 lines, combined with any 4 from the remaining 9 needs 14 x 126 = 1764 lines.

Costs of the example aside:

Vernons - As shown

Littlewoods - £30.24

Zetters - £3.02 (Super Stake)

Brittens - £1.21

ENTRIES OF 18 SELECTIONS

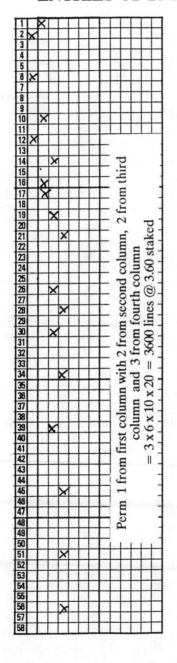

43758 lines are needed to fully cover 8 from 18. The example aside shows a "split group" approach which is capable of many variations, e.g. groups of 5, 6, 7 or whatever. In such approaches careful division of your total selections is wise, particularly when one of the groups is small or when you look to a group to provide the majority of correct results.

Example costs are:

Zetters - As shown

Littlewoods - £36.00

Vernons - £10.28

Brittens - £1.44

ENTRIES OF 18 SELECTIONS

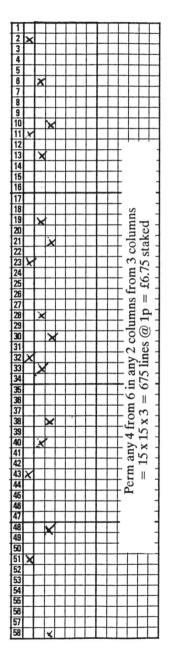

In this example, 18 matches are split into 3 groups of 6. Taking any 4 from 6 in any 2 columns provides full cover for each combination at a reasonable cost, i.e.

Littlewoods - As shown

Vernons - £1.93

Zetters - 67p (Super stake)

Brittens - 27p

On lower cost pools, multiple entries are possible, e.g. by adding another group of 6, the calculation is doubled and so also is the cost.

And for 5 groups of 6 the calculation becomes 15 x 15 x 10 = 2250 lines.

ENTRIES OF 18 SELECTIONS

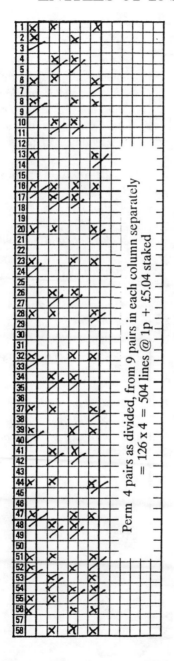

Perm 4 pairs as divided, from 9 pairs in each column separately = 126 x 4 = 504 lines @ 1p + £5.04 staked

An approach based on pairs only, and capable of extension according to your pool and staking limits. In the example shown, note that some matches appear twice and others, three times. Careful distribution of your "strong" selections is therefore needed, if you follow this approach. Whatever your make-up of pairs, you need 4 of them to be correct in one column to qualify for the major prize.

Example costs are:

Littlewoods - As shown

Vernons - £1.44

Zetters - 50p (Super Stake)

Brittens - 21p (Rounded)

ENTRIES OF 18 SELECTIONS

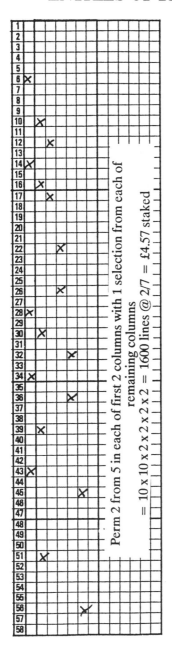

Perm 2 from 5 in each of first 2 columns with 1 selection from each of remaining columns

$= 10 \times 10 \times 2 \times 2 \times 2 \times 2 \times 2 = 1600 \text{ lines @ } 2/7 = £4.57 \text{ staked}$

This example shows a relatively cheap way of covering 18 selections and can be adapted to various combinations depending on how you want to split your total matches, e.g. 6 in one column and 6 sets of 2 each in other columns. Taking 2 from the group of 6, with any 1 from each of the remaining columns = 15 x 2 x 2 x 2 x 2 x 2 x 2 = 960 lines.

For the example aside, costs are:

Vernons - As shown

Littlewoods - £16.00

Zetters - £1.60 (Super Stake)

Brittens - 64p

ENTRIES OF 19 SELECTIONS

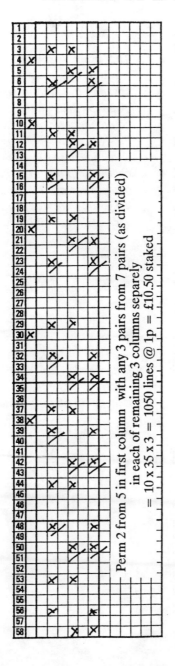

Perm 2 from 5 in first column with any 3 pairs from 7 pairs (as divided) in each of remaining 3 columns separely

= 10 x 35 x 3 = 1050 lines @ 1p = £10.50 staked

75582 lines are needed to fully cover 8 from 19 selections. Even with other approaches, it is difficult to avoid high cost and retain a reasonable chance of success. For multiple entries, a group or syndicate cost-sharing effort may be the best way to proceed. In the example (aside), 26 numbers are split into a group of 5, and 7 pairs in each of 3 columns, with 3 matches making up each set of 3 pairs, reading across the 3 columns. Any 2 Score Draws in any set of 3 matches must be paired in one of the 3 columns. If this occurs 3 times, with all 3 pairs in one column and you have 2 correct in your 1st column, you must be in the money.

Costs:

Littlewoods - As shown

Vernons - £3.00

Zetters - £1.05 (Super Stake)

Brittens - 42p

ENTRIES OF 19 SELECTIONS

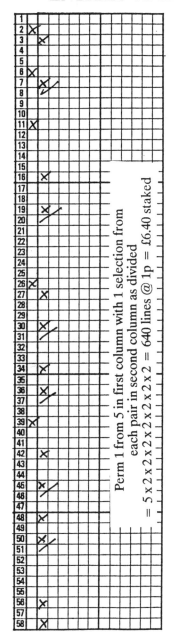

A variation on the previous example, this costs much less and on the cheaper pools is easily capable of varied or multiple entries. Choose and split your selections with care; remember that apart from needing 1 correct in your 1st column, you also need 1 correct in every pair. If your pairs do not conveniently fall into the pattern as shown, enter each of them in a separate column. Amended instructions: "Perm 1 from 5 in 1st Column with 1 selection from each pair in remaining 7 columns. The calculation part of your instructions is of course unchanged.

Costs:

Littlewoods - As shown

Vernons - £1.83

Zetters - 64p (Super Stake)

Brittens - 26p (Rounded)

ENTRIES OF 19 SELECTIONS

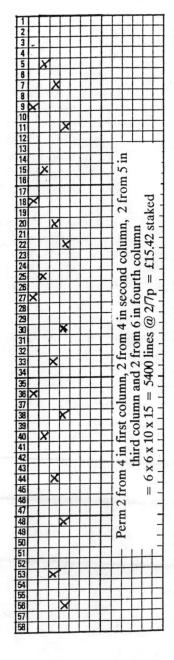

Perm 2 from 4 in first column, 2 from 4 in second column, 2 from 5 in third column and 2 from 6 in fourth column = 6 x 6 x 10 x 15 = 5400 lines @ 2/7p = £15.42 staked

For syndicates or "Family Groups", a split approach may be the answer, if selections are well chosen, and a measure of Full Cover is required. There are - obviously - many ways of splitting 19 selections, e.g. into 3 groups of 5 and 6 and 8, or a group of 4 with 3 groups of 5, etc. I repeat (without apology) that in such entries, care is also required in making up the individual groups, i.e., the smaller groups should ideally contain the most "Confident" selections. This general rule must of course be treated with common sense; if you are looking to 6 or 7 selections to provide 4 Score-Draws, then you need good selections in such groups. If on the other hand, you are seeking one result from 5 matches, you need a lower degree of optimism.

The example aside costs:

Vernons - As shown

Littlewoods - £54.00

Zetters - £5.49 (Super Stake)

Brittens - £2.16

ENTRIES OF 19 SELECTIONS

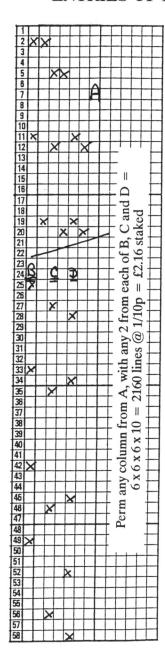

Perm any column from A, with any 2 from each of B, C and D = 6 x 6 x 6 x 10 = 2160 lines @ 1/10p = £2.16 staked

One way of reducing costs to an acceptable level is to cover some selections with a Block method already explained on earlier pages. In this example, the same groupings are used as are given on the previous page, i.e. 2 groups of 4, 1 group of 5 and 1 of 6. The difference is that the 6 match element is covered by a Block of 6 lines guaranteeing 2 Score-Draws if 3 such results occur in the 6 selections. The other groups (of 4 and 5) are dealt with exactly as in the previous example.

Note that - as with all blocks - the chosen matches can of course be spread down the coupon, or be confined to one area of the coupon, as aside.

Costs:

Zetters - As shown (Super Stake)

Littlewoods - £21.60

Vernons - £6.17

Brittens - 86p

ENTRIES OF 20 SELECTIONS

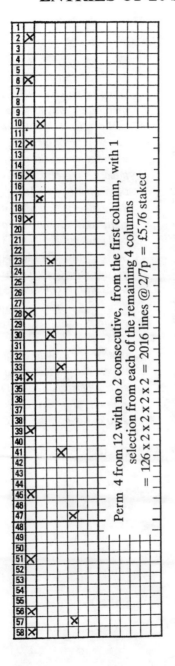

Perm 4 from 12 with no 2 consecutive, from the first column, with 1 selection from each of the remaining 4 columns

$= 126 \times 2 \times 2 \times 2 \times 2 = 2016$ lines @ 2/7p = £5.76 staked

A useful way of dealing with 20 selections (or any other large batch of numbers) is to cover some of them with a non-consecutive permutation. The example aside requires 4 successes to fall into a non-consecutive pattern, with 1 correct result in each of the remaining 4 pairs. This type of entry is clearly capable of variation in both the numbers of matches to be treated as non-consecutive, and how the remainder are to be covered. If you want to cover all 20 as non-consecutive, the instruction would read "Perm 8 from 20 with no 2 consecutive selections = 1287 lines" (add the cost etc.)

The example (aside) costs:

Vernons - As shown

Littlewoods - £20.16

Zetters - £2.01 (Super Stake)

Brittens - 81p (Rounded)

ENTRIES OF 20 SELECTIONS

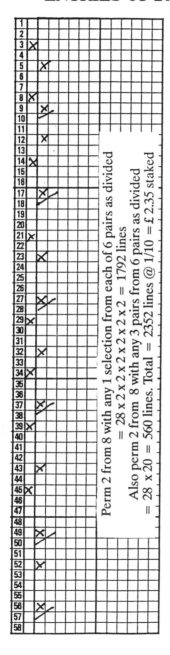

Perm 2 from 8 with any 1 selection from each of 6 pairs as divided
= 28 x 2 x 2 x 2 x 2 x 2 x 2 = 1792 lines

Also perm 2 from 8 with any 3 pairs from 6 pairs as divided
= 28 x 20 = 560 lines. Total = 2352 lines @ 1/10 = £ 2.35 staked

Double cover versions are popular with some people. In the example aside, you have 8 matches in which to find 2 Score draws; therefore the more confident selections should go into the 6 pairs. The latter are covered both ways, i.e. for 1 correct result in each pair, and for 3 correct pairs out of the 6. And you can of course vary the number of selections to be treated as pairs or otherwise, with appropriate alterations to the instructions.

Example costs are:

Zetters - as shown (Super Stake)

Littlewoods - £23.52

Vernons - £6.72

Brittens - 94p

ENTRIES OF 20 SELECTIONS

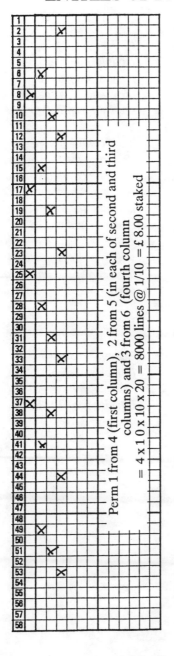

Perm 1 from 4 (first column), 2 from 5 (in each of second and third columns) and 3 from 6 (fourth column

= 4 x 1 0 x 10 x 20 = 8000 lines @ 1/10 = £8.00 staked

This type of split group approach can be quite expensive, but on lower cost pools is within scope for family groups or syndicates. With 20 selections, there is a wide variety of combinations of 3 or 4 groups which might suit your needs, but do work out the cost, take care with your overall selections and the way you split them into smaller groups.

Example costs:

Zetters - as shown (Super Stake)

Littlewoods - £80.00

Vernons - £22.86

Brittens - £3.20

ENTRIES OF 20 SELECTIONS

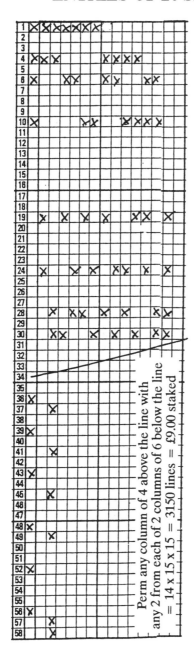

Perm any column of 4 above the line with
any 2 from each of 2 columns of 6 below the line
= 14 x 15 x 15 = 3150 lines = £9.00 staked

In this example, 8 matches are covered by a 14 column block, ensuring that if 5 are correct in the 8, then 4 must be on one line in the block of 14 columns. 12 other matches are split into 2 groups of 6, with a requirement that any 2 be taken from both groups. Again, the variety of block entries possible with 20 selections, is quite wide and for those who like this approach, the entire 20 matches could be covered by mixed block entries (see earlier examples of various blocks). For space reasons, the example shows the 8 match block covering numbers in the top half of the coupon. It could of course be spread down the coupon just as easily.

Example costs:

Vernons - as shown

Littlewoods - £31.50

Zetters - £3.15 (Super Stake)

Brittens - £1.26

LARGER ENTRIES - MIXED APPROACHES

21 SELECTIONS

Full Cover for all 21 is out of the question because more than 200,000 lines are needed to provide it. Even with 3 groups of 7 matches, taking any 4 from each of any 2 groups, the calculation shows that 3675 lines are required (35 x 35 x 3). This is however much more acceptable on cost terms, and for those who feel confident enough to try it, the stakes are:

Littlewoods -	£36.75	Adding a 4th Group of 7
Vernons -	£10.50	Doubles the calculation
Zetters -	£3.67	and the cost, i.e. any 2
	(Super Stake)	groups of 7 from 4 groups
Brittens -	£1.47	= 6 entries.

21 Selections can of course be split in many other ways, producing varied results according to the mix of groups you use. If - for example, you choose to go for groups of 6, 7 and 8, taking any 4 from any 2 groups, the result is:

4 from 6 with 4 from 7 = 15 x 35 = 525	Total
4 from 6 with 4 from 8 = 15 x 70 = 1025	4025
4 from 7 with 4 from 8 = 35 x 70 = 2450	lines

At just over 4000 lines, this may be within scope for individuals on lower cost pools, or for syndicates/family groups on Vernons, or for large syndicates on Littlewoods.

Is it worth exploring other group combinations? If you want to retain full cover, the answer is probably no. Groups of 5, 7 and 9, with 2 from 5, 3 from 7 and 3 from 9, result in over 29000 lines. So it is worth looking at **other** ways, of dealing with 21 selections, by using mixed approaches covering various groups of numbers.

LARGER ENTRIES : MIXED APPROACHES

21 SELECTIONS

Pairs - on their own - are out for obvious reasons. But if some matches are taken in a group to be covered in other ways, the remainder can be dealt with as pairs providing you leave an even number. Examples:

1. Any 2 from 5, with any 3 pairs from 8 pairs = 560 lines.

2. Any 2 from 7 with any 1 selection from any 6 pairs from 7 pairs = 21 x 2 x 2 x 2 x 2 x 2 x 2 (x 7) = 9408 lines.

3. Any 4 from 9 with any 2 pairs from 6 pairs = 1890 lines.

The above are a few simple examples of mixing pairs and full cover. Switching to pairs and non-consecutives: (Examples)

4. Any 2 pairs from 5 pairs, with any 4 from 11. (No 2 consecutive selections) = 10 x 70 = 700 lines.

5. Any 1 selection from each of 4 pairs, with any 4 from 13 (No 2 consecutive selections) = 2 x 2 x 2 x 2 x 210 = 3360 lines.

6. Any 3 pairs from 6 pairs, with any 2 from 9 (No 2 consecutive selections) = 20 x 28 = 560 lines. (Changing this to any 1 selection from each of 6 pairs with any 2 from 9 (No 2 consecutive selections becomes 2 x 2 x 2 x 2 x 2 x 2 x 28 = 1792 lines).

Clearly some of the above examples could easily become multiple entries of either the same 21 selections or a larger total suitably split into manageable groups. And of course other variations are possible with this as with any other mix of approaches, e.g.

7. Any 2 pairs from 4 pairs, with any 1 selection from each of 3 pairs, with any 3 from 7 (no 2 consecutive selections) = 6 x 2 x 2 x 2 x 10 = 480 lines. Again, this mix can be varied according to the numbers used in each part of the entry, but do make sure that your 21 selections are all included, and that you have allowed for 8 Score Draws, with clear division of groups of numbers and equally clear instructions.

LARGER ENTRIES : MIXED APPROACHES

22 SELECTIONS

This is a nice round number, representing nearly 38% of the total of 58 matches on the coupon. So even with random selections, you could expect to find about 4 Score Draws on an average week. The idea of course is not to find 4, but 8, because the former puts your money into someone else's dividend, and the latter (8) brings the dividend to you if you have them all in one line of your entry.

Even with split groups, Full Cover by itself is very costly:

4 from 11 with 4 from 11 = 330 x 330 = 108900. And:

4 from 12 with 4 from 10 = 495 x 210 = 103950. To cut this short, the lowest reasonable combination, i.e. any 4 from 6 with any 4 from 16 works out at 15 x 1820 = 27300 lines.

How about trying Blocks and Full Cover? Reference back to the pages with the numbered Blocks will remind you that various numbers of matches can be covered by comparatively few lines if the conditions are acceptable, e.g. that in order to guarantee 2 on a line there must 3 correct in the total. Splitting your 22 selections into groups of 7, 7, and 8 respectively, means that you could for example have:

1. Block 3 covering each of the 2 groups of 7, with any 4 from 8, = 9 x 9 x 70 = 5670 lines.

2. Block 3 covering 7 matches, Block 8 covering 8 matches, with any 3 from 7 = 9 x 20 x 35 = 6300 lines.

3. Block 7 covering each of 2 groups of 7, with any 2 from 8 = 12 x 12 x 28 = 4032 lines.

With this mix of approaches, you need to decide how many matches you want to fully cover, and which combination of blocks to use on the remaining matches. The cheapest combination is 3 groups of 6 matches, each covered by Block 2, with any 2 from the remaining 4 matches (6 x 6 x 6 x 6 = 1296 lines).

LARGER ENTRIES : MIXED APPROACHES

22 SELECTIONS

Mixing block and non-consecutive approaches may appeal to some readers, particularly those who find conditional guarantees acceptable, since both methods are within this description. As to cost, this will depend on your split of selections, i.e. how many to cover with the block method and how many to be dealt with as non-consecutive. If for example you choose to use Blocks 2, or 3, or 4, with the remaining 16, or 15, or 14 matches covered by Non-Consecutive perms, the results are:

4. 6 matches covered by Block 2, with Any 6 non-consecutive selections from 16 matches = 6 x 462 = 2772 lines.

5. 7 matches covered by Block 3, with Any 6 non-consecutive selections from 15 matches = 9 x 210 = 1890 lines.

6. 8 matches covered by Block 4, with any 6 non-consecutive selections from 14 matches = 12 x 84 = 1008 lines.

Even though the above examples result in considerably reduced expense, they are perhaps best suited to lower cost pools, unless you belong to a group or syndicate where the total stake is shared.

Balance is clearly important in this mix of approaches. In example 6 above, 6 non-consecutive selections in 14 matches is exactly the same as Full Cover for any 6 from 9, which even for an "Expert" forecaster, may seem like a tall order. In other words, if you decide to use an approach of this type, careful forecasting coupled with sensible grouping of your selections is a must. Yes I'm well aware that I've said that a few times, but no apologies for repeating it. Avoid wasting your selections by being careless with the grouping aspect; the more you want from a group, the greater the need to put your best selections into it. And then make sure that your perm or other cover is reasonable, because the point of it all is to have a fair chance of winning.

LARGER ENTRIES : MIXED APPROACHES

24 SELECTIONS

No, that is not a misprint. I am trying - in these pages - to give examples rather than to cover every number of selections. So before the "Action Group for 23 selections" starts to organise protests or to lobby their MP's or whatever, let me say that their time would be better spent exercising their minds as to what they consider the best way to handle their favourite number.

24 selections fairly easily breaks down into manageable groups:

> 12 Pairs or 2 sets of 12 selections;
>
> 8 Groups of 3, or 3 groups of 8;
>
> 6 Groups of 4, or 4 groups of 6;
>
> 3 Groups of 7, 8 and 9 selections respectively, and various other combinations.

Some of the above combinations can be dealt with under Full Cover only. Examples would include:

- Any 4 Pairs from 12 Pairs = 495 lines, easily capable of multiple entries on cheaper pools, using different mixes of pairs for each entry.

- Any 1 from each of 8 groups of 3 = 3 x 3 x 3 x 3 x 3 x 3 x 3 x 3 = 6561 lines (£18.75 on Vernons, £6.56 on Zetters, 2.62 on Brittens).

If we try a mixed approach of pairs and blocks, some examples are worth mentioning:

1. Any 2 pairs from 5 pairs, with two groups of 7 matches, each covered by block 3 = 10 x 9 x 9 = 810 lines (Cheap but ambitious!)

2. Any 1 selection from any 4 pairs (of 5 pairs), with 2 groups of 7 matches each covered by block 3 = 2 x 2 x 2 x 2 (x 5) x 9 x 9 = 6480 lines.

3. Any 1 selection from each of any 4 pairs (of 8 pairs), with the remaining 8 matches covered by Block 12 = 2 x 2 x 2 x 2 (x 70) x 14 = 15680 lines.

Example 3 above is very costly; simplifying it into any 2 pairs from 8 (28 lines) with the remaining 8 matches covered by Block 3, reduces it to 28 x 14 = 392 lines which loses much flexibility but is very cheap. You get what you are willing to pay for!

Fortunately, there are other possibilities. The single Block approach, i.e. using the same block to cover all groups of selections is feasible with 24 matches. Block 12 covers 8 numbers in 14 columns and ensures that if your 8 selections contain 5 correct results, 4 of them must be brought together on one of the 14 columns. Therefore:

4. Any 2 groups of 8 matches (from 3 groups), with all groups covered by block 12 = 14 x 14 x 3 = 588 lines. Cheap, and multiple entries on cheaper pools are a real possibility.

Mixing the blocks is also within reason:

5. Any 2 groups of 8 selections each covered by Block 8, with the remaining 8 selections covered by Block 4 = 20 x 20 x 12 = 4800 lines.

LARGER ENTRIES: MIXED APPROACHES

24 SELECTIONS

The above are only a few examples of using blocks with other blocks to cover your 24 selections. All blocks have to be entered in full on the coupon with clear separation lines and indicators, e.g. if using 3 blocks, mark them A, B, and C on your coupon and refer to them as such in your instructions (unless of course all blocks are the same, when it is only necessary to take any column from each of any 2 blocks or whatever). Do your blocks on a spare coupon first, make sure they are correct, give plain instructions and - hopefully - wait for the cheque to arrive.

LARGER ENTRIES : MIXED APPROACHES

25 SELECTIONS

An obvious way of dealing with 25 selections is to split them into 5 groups of 5 and take any 2 selections from any 4 groups. It may be obvious; it is also costly, i.e. $10 \times 10 \times 10 \times 10 \ (\times 5) = 50000$ lines, or £20 even on the cheapest pool.

Mixing Full Cover and non-consecutive approaches does not reduce costs sufficiently, e.g. Any 2 from 9, with any 3 from each of two groups of 8 (No 2 consecutive in either group) = $36 \times 20 \times 20 = 14400$ lines. But if we return to the 5 groups of 5 and take a similar approach:

1. Perm any 2 from 5 in 1st column, with any 2 non consecutive selections from each of any 3 remaining columns, the result is $10 \times 6 \times 6 \times 6 \ (\times 4) = 8640$ lines. Your 1st group is fully covered; all other groups depend on 2 score draws falling non-consecutively. If you change the requirements (but still using 5 groups of 5) you might for example get:

2. Perm any 3 from 5 in 1st column, with any 3 from 5 in 2nd column, and any 2 non consecutive selections in any 1 remaining column = $10 \times 10 \times 6 \ (\times 3)$ 1800 lines. In this example, a lot of weight rests on your first two groups, which therefore need your best selections.

If you really fancy your chances at forecasting, you could try any 4 from 5 in one column, with any 2 from each of any remaining 2 groups of 5. With 5 columns of 5, the calculation is $5 \times 10 \times 10 \ (\times 6) = 3000$ lines (£8.57 on Vernons). But if you like a mix of full cover and non consecutive:

3. Perm any 2 from 10 in 1st column, with any 2 non consecutive selections from each of any 2 remaining columns. The result is: $45 \times 6 \times 6 \ (\times 3) = 4860$ lines (£4.86 on Zetters).

In this example, you would of course need only 4 columns in all with 10 in the 1st and 5 in each of the other 3.

What everyone would like is to cover 25 selections for the lowest possible cost. How about 10 pence - is that low enough for you? When the cries of disbelief and derision die down, I'll tell you how to do it. Your chances of winning may be slim, but if you are full of confidence, all you have to do is:

Split your 25 selections into the ever popular 5 groups of 5. Write your instructions: "Perm Any 4 from 5 in any 2 groups = 5 x 5 x 10 = 250 lines = 10p staked (on Brittens Pools at 25 lines a penny). You will of course have to make extra entries to meet the minimum stake requirements. And think of the multiple entry possibilities.....

Other alternatives:

4 Split your 25 selections into 2 groups of 8 and 1 of 9. Use Block 12 to cover each group of 8 and Block 13 to cover the group of 9. With 5 Score Draws in each of any 2 groups, you must have a line of 8. The calculation: 14 x 14 = 196, plus 14 x 30 (x 2) = 840. Total = 1036 lines.

5. Make 6 selections into 3 pairs. Cover 2 other groups of 6 with Block 2 and 1 group of 7 with Block 3. The calculation is: Any 1 selection from each of any 2 pairs (of 3 pairs) = 2 x 2 (x 3) = 12 x 6 x 6 x 9 = 3888 lines.

6. Put 5 selections in one group. Put 6 selections into 3 pairs, and cover the remaining 14 selections with two entries of Block 3. Any 1 from 5, with any 1 selection from each of 3 pairs (= 5 x 8 = 40) x 9 x 9 = 3240 lines.

Blocks can help to reduce costs, but continuation sheets will be necessary for the larger blocks. These sheets can be obtained free from your Pools firm.

LARGER ENTRIES : MIXED APPROACHES

27 SELECTIONS

Assuming that you are not interested in an entry of over 2 million lines to provide Full Cover for all 27 matches, two other simple "splits" are:

Three groups of 9, taking any 4 from each of any 2 groups = 126 x 126 (x 3) = 47628 lines . Quite costly but cheaper than 9 groups of 3 taking any 1 selection from each of any 8 groups = 3 x 3 x 3 x 3 x 3 x 3 x 3 x 3 (x 9) = 59049 lines.

If your confidence is **really** high, you could use the 9 groups of 3 approach, but go for any 2 from each of any 4 groups. The calculation is 3 x 3 x 3 x 3 (x 126) = 10206 lines.

Using non-consecutive calculations, with 3 groups of 9 reduces the cost to more acceptable levels,i.e.

1. Any 4 non-consecutive selections from each of any 2 groups = 15 x 15 (x 3) = 675 lines.
The block approach, (using Block 13) with 3 groups of 9 is more expensive than Example 1:

2. 30 x 30 (x 3) = 2700 lines. With 5 correct in any 2 groups, you are certain of a line with 8 together.
Mixing the block and non-consecutive approaches, still with 3 groups of 9 results in:
3. Any 4 non-consecutive selections from any group of 9 with any column from Block 13 covering either of the other 2 groups = 2700 lines.
By adding in the extra cover provided by Example 2 above, the total becomes 5400 lines.
In entries of this type, groups of 9 to be covered non-consecutively and the 30 lines of Block 3, have to be entered separately for each calculation, i.e. 3 columns of 9 and 3 Block 13 entries, with clear instructions.

By now, you know why larger blocks are not so popular. They are time-consuming to enter, they may require continuation sheets and you need to be precise in linking them with other methods of entry when you write your instructions. On the other hand, they provide fair guarantees and reduce costs quite drastically. The choice is yours. The many people who have won dividends using Block type entries will swear by them; others may want to swear at them!

Other mixed approaches may be tried, but none are likely to be low in cost. Mixing Full Cover, non-consecutives and Pairs is possible with various combinations of numbers:

4. Any 2 from 5 (Full Cover) with any 2 non-consecutive selections from each of 2 groups of 7 selections and any 1 pair from 4 pairs = $10 \times 15 \times 15 \times 4$ = 9000 lines.

For a simpler, less costly approach but one which depends on your skill at forecasting pairs, you could try:

5. Any 3 pairs from 11 pairs with any 2 from 5 = 165×10 = 1650 lines. Variations (and possibly multiple entries) are feasible with this approach, e.g. any 3 pairs from 10 pairs with any 2 from 7 = 120×21 = 2520 lines.

An acquaintance - who has some good fortune with "Bankers" i.e. matches he regards as certainties for a draw result - uses a simple entry on a low cost pool:

6. Any 2 from each of any 3 groups of 5 (from 5 groups) with 2 Banker selections = $10 \times 10 \times 10 \ (\times 10) \times 1$ = 10000 lines. Using 3 Bankers (and looking for 2 to be right) with any 3 from any 2 groups of 6 (from 4 groups) produces:

$20 \times 20 \ (\times 6) \times 3$ = 7200 lines. If 2 of your Bankers are correct, careful checking of your other groups is well worth the effort.

LARGER ENTRIES : MIXED APPROACHES

28 SELECTIONS

With such a large number of selections - almost half the coupon - virtually any form of entry will be costly. For the Full Cover enthusiast, this will apply to any split of the 28 matches. The split which most commonly springs to mind is the good old 4 groups of 7. Using this as a basis for Full Cover.

Any 2 from each of 4 groups of $7 = 21 \times 21 \times 21 \times 21 = 194481$ lines, which is beyond any reasonable limit.

What about the opposite grouping, i.e. 7 groups of 4? With only 7 groups, 2 selections must come from 1 group, with 1 from each of the remaining groups (of 4). The calculation is $6 \times 4 \times 4 \times 4 \times 4 \times 4 \times 4 = 24576$ lines, which is still very costly even on low stake pools. The cost can of course be reduced if 3 selections are taken from any two groups of 4, with 2 selections from one group only, i.e.:

1. Any 2 selections from the first column, with any 3 selections from each of any 2 remaining columns. The calculation is: $6 \times 4 \times 4 \ (\times 15) = 1440$ lines. This is much more reasonable in cost terms (£4.11p on Vernons) but of course is also quite optimistic in seeking to get 3 correct in each of two groups of 4 selections.

2. Taking 2 groups of 8 and 2 groups of 6, with 3 non-consecutives in each of the first 2 groups and 2 non-consecutives from either of the last 2 groups, produces what for some people may be an acceptable cost on cheaper pools, i.e.:

Any 3 non-consecutive selections from each of the first 2 columns, with any 2 non-consecutive selections from either of the 2 remaining columns = $20 \times 20 \times 10 \ (\times 2) = 8000$ lines.

3. From the pairs viewpoint, the simplest entry would be:

Any 4 pairs from 14 pairs = 1001 lines (£2.86 on Vernons, £1.00 on Zetters Super Stake and only 40 pence on Brittens). You may well need strong forecasting and pairing ability to make this a success, but with multiple entries a real possibility on lower cost pools, you may want to consider it.

Variation is possible with the Pairs approach. For low cost entries (and high optimism!), two sets of 4 pairs and one set of 6 pairs produces:

Any 2 pairs from each group of 4 pairs, with any 2 pairs from 6 pairs in the third group = 6 x 6 x 15 = 540 lines. I prefer a different grouping for this "Fingers Crossed" approach, i.e. 2 groups of 5 pairs and 1 of 4 pairs:

4. Any 3 pairs from either of 2 groups of 5 pairs, with any 1 pairs from the third group = 10 x 4 (x 2) = 80 lines.

For the block approach, costs rise again, e.g. Block 3 (covering 7 matches) used 4 times = 6561 lines.

Mixing pairs and blocks - as approaches - reduces outlay but increases the "Luck" factor. Two examples:

5. Any 2 pairs from 7 pairs, with 2 entries of Block 3, produces 21 x 9 x 9 = 1701 lines.

6. Any 2 pairs from 6 pairs, with 2 entries of Block 4 gives 15 x 12 x 12 = 2160 lines.

As with all examples, you can ring the changes by using other combinations and mixes of different approaches to suit your needs and your pocket.

LARGER ENTRIES : MIXED APPROACHES

30 SELECTIONS

At this level, we are taking over half the coupon (51.7%), meaning that on average, about 5 Score Draws should be found in the 30 matches. Sensible use of the Tables given earlier, should help to improve that measure of success. But of course there is still the problem of getting 8 together on one line of the entry. To illustrate the Full Cover costs: (using 3 groups of 10 matches). Any 4 from each of any 2 groups of 10 selections = 210 x 210 (x 3) = 132300 lines. If you can smile and sleep easily while paying for that every week of the season, why are you doing the pools at all?

Splitting your 30 selections into 6 groups of 5 and taking any 2 from each of any 4 groups is even worse at 150000 lines. And over 253000 lines are needed with 5 groups of 6, taking any 2 from each of any 4 groups.

Can anything be done to limit this type of mind-boggling result? Some limitation is possible, if the cost and the perm structure are acceptable, e.g. (using 6 groups of 5).

1. Any 2 from the 1st column, with any 3 from each of any 2 of the remaining 5 columns = 10 x 10 x 10 (x 10) = 10000 lines.

Switching to non-consecutives reduces the above to more acceptable levels. Using 3 groups of 10:

2. Any 4 non-consecutive selections from each of any 2 groups: = 35 x 35 (x 3) = 3675 lines.

Using 3 varied groups, such as 9, 10, and 11 respectively, taking any 4 non consecutive form each of any 2 groups produces a very similar result, i.e. 4025 lines (15 x 35 = 525, plus 15 x 70 = 1050, plus 35 x 70 = 2450, total 4025).

3. With 15 pairs available in 30 matches, any 4 pairs from 15 pairs = 1365 lines may suit you if you are keen on this approach.

With the block type approach, the simplest version is to make 5 groups of 6, each covered by Block 2. Taking any column from each of any 4 Blocks produces 6 x 6 x 6 x 6 (x 5) = 6480 lines. This really does require a lot of good fortune with results. Alternatives can be found by using other Block combinations e.g. 1 Block 2 (6 matches) and 3 Block 4 (8 matches) entries, taking any column from each Block, i.e. 6 x 12 x 12 x 12 = 10368 lines.

With your best 6 selections covered by block 2, and with 3 separate block 8 entries (each guaranteeing 3 together if 4 are correct in the 8), the calculation becomes:

4. Any column in first Block with any column from each of any 2 remaining Blocks = 6 x 20 x 20 (x 3) = 7200 lines.

5. And if you really like Blocks and don't mind the punishment, Block 13 combined with 3 entries of Block 3 provides:

Any column from 1st block, with any column from any 2 remaining blocks, i.e. 30 x 9 x 9 (x 3) = 7290 lines in all.

If you want a mixed bag of approaches, there are lots of options open to you, but most of them are very costly. And simple entries are much easier to check let alone to fill in on the coupon. However, you may want to strike a blow for individualism; you could for instance, try:

6. Any 1 from 4 (full cover) with any column from Block 2 (covering 6 matches) with any pair from 5 pairs and any 3 non-consecutive selections from 10 matches. The calculation

is 4 x 6 x 5 x 56 = 6720 lines. At £6.72 on Zetters Super Stake or £2.69 on Brittens, this may appeal to the diehards.

These examples - over the various selection totals - show that on the one hand you need not be tied down to one method of entry, but on the other side of the coin, time and effort are needed when mixed approaches are used.

WAYS AND MEANS

So you would like to cover 35 matches, retain Full Cover and spend as little as possible. Any 2 groups of 5 from 7 groups results in 21 entries of 8 from 10 or 21 x 45 = 945 lines. How to achieve reasonable cover at a lower cost?

Using Block 3 as a base, number your 7 groups of 5 and link the groups as shown in the block, i.e. group 1 is linked to group 4, group 2 to group 6 and so on. When you have 9 such linkages, you have 9 groups of 10 selection with the certainty that 2 of your best 3 groups of 5 must be linked into one of your sets of 10 selections. The cost is of course 9 x 45 = 405 lines instead of the 945 referred to above.

In the same way, 40 selections can be dealt with by using block 4, i.e. 8 groups of 5, numbered and linked as per the Block layout. You will then have 12 sets of 10 selections with the same guarantee which is that 2 of your best 3 groups of 5 must be together in one set of 10. Cost is 45 x 12 = 540 lines, affordable on all pools.

You can of course use other selection totals and other Blocks. To cover 12 matches fully (for any 8) needs 495 lines. You have - let us say - 28 selections. Using block 7, link 7 groups of 4 as per the block layout, i.e. the first group of 4 is linked to the third and the sixth (making 12 selections), the fourth group is linked to the sixth and seventh (making another set of 12 selections) and so on. When finished the linking process you will have 12 columns of 12 selections and the knowledge that 3 of your best 4 groups must be together in one of your 12 columns. The cost is 12 x 495 = 5940 lines, affordable on cheaper pools.

The same process can be used with other sets of numbers, or for multiple entries of a (good) conditional guarantee perm or whatever as a means of reducing costs but retaining a defined degree of protection for your entry.

YES BUT ITS FUN ISN'T IT?

You have seen the tables, read or scanned through the examples, perhaps thought about the block or other methods, and you became interested, angry, or amused by the mixed approaches etc. Somewhere along the way, it may be that the going got exciting, or rough or whatever. Bear with me therefore for reminding you that the purposes of this book were:

- To stimulate your interest in identifying potential Score-draws.
- To perhaps persuade you that its not ALL down to luck.
- To show you that a variety of methods can be used for entries.
- To help you reduce the rather massive odds against success.

All of the above are very worthwhile. Even if they are all achieved, a measure of good fortune or luck is still unavoidable. If doing the pools could be reduced to a matter of precise selection and effective permutation cover at a reasonable cost, plus the certainty of success, the pools would all close down tomorrow or even today. What I'm saying here is, do your very best with both selections and permutations, but do not spend more than you can afford, do not expect to receive a stream of high dividend cheques (one will do for most of us) and do not take it all too seriously. Keep a sense of perspective, be persistent with your entry and be patient. Doing the pools can be fun and particularly so when you check the results on Saturday and realise that 8 of your selections are Score-Draws. Are they all in one line of your entry? Will your perm guarantee this? How many Score-draws are there in all among the 58 matches? How big will the dividend be? And who are you going to tell first? As for the begging letters, well when I discussed that aspect with my better half, she told me to keep sending them out.....

APPENDIX

*The following pages show a revised layout for Table Six,
as at the end of 1990-1991 Season.*

Table Six (Updated)

Draw ratings for teams alphabetically

Note:- Ratings are an assessment of draw potential. Low ratings are "best" for draw results at home or away as applicable. Some team have equal ratings in one or more columns.

Home				Away		
All Draws	No Score Draws	Score Draws	Teams	Score Draws	No Score Draws	All Draws
7	6	9	Aberdeen	1	8	2
5	6	7	Airdrie	2	1	1
6	5	6	Aldershot	14	13	17
11	4	12	Arsenal	13	2	9
13	8	11	Aston Villa	4	14	5
5	6	9	Barnsley	3	7	3
6	1	16	Birmingham	3	9	1
10	14	7	Blackburn	1	15	5
14	8	12	Blackpool	2	9	1
13	6	15	Bolton	11	9	12
10	6	12	Bournemouth	12	4	7
2	7	4	Bradford City	2	13	1
7	15	2	Brentford	7	10	6
9	8	11	Brighton	17	9	15
14	10	14	Bristol City	8	3	5
1	5	4	Bristol Rovers	10	7	9
10	4	13	Burnley	12	5	11
4	4	7	Bury	1	18	3
17	13	14	Cambridge	9	2	3
5	1	11	Cardiff	19	1	12
13	11	8	Carlisle	16	8	16
7	9	6	Celtic	7	7	9
7	6	11	Charlton	10	13	13
5	7	6	Chelsea	7	12	6

TABLE SIX (UPDATED)

Draw ratings for teams (alphabetically)

Home				Away		
All Draws	No Score Draws	Score Draws		Score Draws	No Score Draws	All Draws
14	7	15	Chester	10	16	15
15	2	15	Chesterfield	8	5	7
16	1	17	Coventry	15	1	6
1	9	1	Crewe	15	15	16
9	4	10	Crystal Palace	12	8	12
15	10	11	Darlington	7	5	5
6	9	4	Derby	9	10	7
3	13	2	Doncaster	4	14	9
4	1	7	Dundee Utd.	3	2	3
1	3	1	Dunfermline	2	6	5
3	6	5	Everton	6	13	6
8	11	5	Exeter	5	11	5
7	8	8	Falkirk	3	2	3
12	12	7	Fulham	6	11	6
11	6	12	Gillingham	6	12	10
12	6	14	Grimsby	7	7	4
7	4	9	Halifax	18	11	18
4	7	4	Hartlepool	11	15	15
3	7	2	Hearts	3	1	1
11	3	14	Hereford	9	5	8
2	2	3	Hibernians	2	4	4
9	9	9	Huddersfield	10	9	11
3	3	14	Hull	7	1	2
16	15	13	Ipswich	4	13	8
12	3	14	Leeds United	2	3	1
11	17	5	Leicester	9	14	12

TABLE SIX (UPDATED)

Draw ratings for teams (alphabetically)

All Draws	No Score Draws	Score Draws		Score Draws	No Score Draws	All Draws
14	13	9	Leyton Orient	5	12	5
9	3	12	Lincoln	10	2	6
17	12	16	Liverpool	3	6	2
1	2	4	Luton	13	7	13
18	17	16	Maidstone	21	17	20
12	12	7	Manchester City	16	5	14
8	5	9	Manchester Utd.	3	6	2
7	8	6	Mansfield	9	1	2
4	1	16	Middlesbrough	18	2	14
2	11	3	Millwall	14	4	10
5	8	4	Motherwell	4	9	8
12	9	13	Newcastle	5	5	4
15	12	10	Northampton	16	6	15
4	2	8	Norwich	14	8	15
6	2	15	Notts County	8	8	8
10	4	11	Notts Forest	8	10	6
3	18	1	Oldham	11	6	9
2	14	2	Oxford	12	10	11
8	6	8	Peterborough	3	3	3
7	10	6	Plymouth	6	11	8
6	4	14	Port Vale	2	2	1
15	12	13	Portsmouth	10	7	9
11	2	19	Preston	8	14	10
14	6	15	Queens Park Rangers	17	4	16
6	5	8	Rangers	3	3	4
2	10	3	Reading	13	10	13
2	1	5	Rochdale	4	8	4

TABLE SIX (UPDATED)

Draw ratings for teams (alphabetically)

All Draws	No Score Draws	Score Draws	Teams	Score Draws	No Score Draws	All Draws
6	4	9	Rotherham	8	5	3
5	4	6	St. Johnstone	5	6	7
4	3	5	St. Mirren	6	5	6
17	16	17	Scarborough	20	16	19
1	9	1	Scunthorpe	1	12	2
8	13	6	Sheffield Wed	9	12	10
7	4	9	Sheffield Utd.	11	5	8
3	3	11	Shrewsbury	12	6	10
8	13	1	Southampton	1	11	3
16	9	17	Southend	16	17	17
10	9	7	Stockport	15	4	13
8	8	7	Stoke	15	3	8
2	7	3	Sunderland	10	11	11
16	8	18	Swansea	14	11	14
17	7	17	Swindon	13	2	7
11	14	5	Torquay	10	8	11
15	11	13	Tottenham	10	10	10
18	16	13	Tranmere	3	16	5
3	7	3	Walsall	17	7	17
13	16	8	Watford	16	11	16
4	5	12	West Brom	10	2	6
16	15	13	West Ham	15	5	11
15	14	11	Wigan	4	8	1
3	10	2	Wimbledon	5	9	4
7	7	10	Wolves	8	4	6
12	8	10	Wrexham	5	13	9
16	15	9	York	13	8	14

AND FINALLY

This may be the first Football Pools book you have ever purchased. Quite naturally, I hope that you enjoyed reading it. Beyond that, I also hope that you found something in it to increase your knowledge and to improve your chances of being a dividend winner. If you want to tell me about your success, or to express any other views etc. then please do so.

And finally, whether you are a beginner or an expert on the pools, whether you like or detest some or all of the content of this book, I want to end by sincerely wishing you good fortune with your entries.

May the dividends be with you !

Simon Carrley